THE
CAMBORNE
PLAY

THE CAMBORNE PLAY

A Translation of Beunans Meriasek in verse
by Myrna Combellack

TRURAN

First published in 1988
By Dyllansow Truran
Trewolsta, Trewirgie, Redruth, Cornwall.

Printed and Bound in Kernow by
Troutbeck Press
a subsidiary of R Booth (Bookbinder) Limited
Antron Hill, Mabe, Penryn, Cornwall.   ISBN 1 85022 039 5

This edition was prepared for a performance under the direction of Jerry Finch for the Cornwall Drama Association at the Cornish Eisteddfod, 1986.

Myrna Combellack, Institute of Cornish Studies, Trevenson House, Pool, Redruth, Cornwall, 1985.

CONTENTS

INTRODUCTION

THE Camborne Play was first published in full in 1872 as **The Life of St. Meriasek** or **Beunans Meriasek,** by which name it is known to scholars and students of the Cornish language, also to medieval European dramatists as the only surviving pre-Reformation British saint's play.

The Camborne Play is more than that, however. The whole manuscript, dated 1504, consists of three separate and complete plays, bound together in a logical sequence which merge to form a three-dimensional spectacle over a two-day performance, requiring some 120 players, excluding the requirement for crowds.

Professor Charles Thomas, in his **Christian Antiquities of Camborne,** describes the drama as a many-layered cake; and so it would appear, in this colour-coded edition for schools and dramatists. Each play may be produced on its own or may be incorporated into a full production of the whole manuscript.

I have not added to the stage directions, as I believe that the original medieval dramatist gave fair indication of what he expected from his players, and the 'producer scribe,' who also wrote on the manuscript, did a good job of filling in detailed directions. Modern producers or directors will fill the margins with their own ideas, and my only contribution to that has been to keep the margins sufficiently wide.

I make no apologies for turning the seven-syllabled and four-syllabled rough-hewn Cornish verse (originally written for shouting across an open-air round theatre) into roughly seven- and four-syllabled English doggerel, and offer as my only defence the following:

I have tried to maintain the wordage, the verbiage, the spirit and the content of each speech. Almost without exception, I have managed to maintain the exact number of lines and the exact rhymes and syllable-counts of those individual lines. In order to do this, I have sometimes been unable to translate the actual words appearing in the Cornish.

As a result of these restrictions, it does not surprise me if directors find some lines unspeakable, in both senses of the word. I urge them to re-write such offending lines in production and on the spot, as inspiration takes them: I have found no task associated with the manuscript more creative or rewarding. My only hope is that this translation may have the effect of shedding light upon the Cornish text rather than of obscuring its spirit further. There is little doubt that Camborne's medieval play deserves to be re-played and re-lived, particularly in its home town, wherever and whenever that is possible. It is unique in European drama, and ranks with the finest of its genre.

Students of the Cornish language will have an advantage in being able to study the original text; for this, I would urge consultation of my doctoral thesis, "A Critical Edition of Beunans Meriasek" (Ph.D., University of Exeter, 1985) in which the play is also annotated, and an unactable, but readable translation is offered for greater understanding.

Myrna Combellack
Institute of Cornish Studies
Christmas Eve, 1985.

DRAMATIS PERSONAE with first line numbers

Life of Meriasek

1. Meriasek's Father (1)
2. Meriasek's Mother (17)
3. Meriasek (25)
4. First Messenger (37)
5. The Duke's Squire (70)
6. Master (76)
7. First Scholar (99)
8. Second Scholar (106)
9. King Conan (168)
10. First Lord (181)
11. Second Lord of the King (187)
12. The Duke of Brittany's Spencer (272)
13. The Duke of Orleans (286)
14. The Bishop of Cornouailles (511)
15. Blind Man (534)
16. Cripple (540)
17. Sailor (593)
18. Sailor's Servant (599)
19. Domestic Servant (643)
20. Fever-Patient (678)
21. Cripple (684)
22. A Sick Man (727)
23. Teudar (759)
24. Messenger (767)
25. First Soldier (801)
26. Second Soldier (807)
27. First Torturer (962)
28. Second Torturer (978)
29. Third Torturer (1020)
30. A Menial (1023)
31. Shipmaster (1082)
32. Crewman (1088)
33. A Breton (1103)

34. Constantine (1153)
35. Second Torturer (1186)
36. Third Torturer (1198)
37. Menial (1204)
38. The Earl (1210)
39. First Torturer (1216)
40. A Doctor in the Christian Faith (1222)
41. Jesus (1288)
42. Michael (1294)
43. Gabriel (1300)
44. Silvester (1312)
45. Cardinal (1329)
46. A Justice (1370)
47. Second Messenger (1386)
48. Doctor (1408)
49. Clerk Jenkin (1422)
50. Apollonian Bishop (1428)
51. Prelate (1495)
52. First Mother (1591)
53. Second Mother (1677)
54. Peter (1695)
55. Paul (1701)

Life of Meriasek (in Brittany)

56. First Outlaw (1866)
57. Second Outlaw (1872)
58. Third Outlaw (1884)
59. Merchant (1890)
60. Fourth Outlaw (1902)
61. Priest (1908)
62. Count Rohan (1936)
63. First Messenger (1944)
64. Kinsman of Count Rohan (1956)
65. Kinsman on Meriasek's Father's Side (1974)
66. Fifth Outlaw (2128)

(in Cornwall)

67. The Duke of Cornwall (2205)
68. The Duke's Steward (2224)
69. The Duke's Chamberlain (2229)
70. Second Messenger (2300)
71. First Demon (2326)
72. Beelzebub (2332)

Life of Silvester
Life of Meriasek

73. Earl Globus (2522)
74. The Squire of Earl Globus (2530)
75. The Demoniac (2628)
76. A Deaf Man (2636)
77. The Demon (2650)
78. The Earl of Vannes (2682)
79. A Squire of the Earl of Vannes (2692)
80. The Dean (2704)
81. The Canon (2716)
82. First Messenger (2729)
83. A Cardinal (2769)
84. Bishop of Cornouailles (2860)
85. The Bishop of Cornouaille's Crozier-Bearer (2866)
86. Second Bishop (2872)
87. Second Crozier-Bearer (2878)
88. A Naked, Sick Man (3031)
89. First Leper (3099)
90. Second Leper (3107)
91. Meriasek's Chaplain (3113)

92. King Massen (3156)
93. The King's Hunters (3165)
94. The Woman's Son (3171)
95. The Woman (3179)
96. The Tyrant (3208)
97. First Soldier of the Tyrant (3217)
98. Second Soldier of the Tyrant (3223)
99. The King's Second Hunter (3235)
100. First Torturer (3245)
101. Second Torturer (3251)
102. Third Torturer (3257)
103. The Menial (3281)
104. Demon (Moufras) (3369)
105. Second Demon (Shirlywit) (3376)
106. Third Soldier of the Tyrant (3546)
107. A Jailer (3567)
108. A Boy (3573)
109. First Messenger (3579)
110. Mary (3647)

Life of St. Meriasek

111. A Madman (3803)
112. Head of a Family (3807)

Life of Silvester

113. First Magician Duke (3896)
114. Second Magician Duke (3904)
115. Huntsman (to the Magician Dukes) (3909)
116. Apollonian Bishop (3916)
117. Apollonian Bishop's Crozier-Bearer (3924)
118. Silvester's First Chaplain (4068)
119. Silvester's Second Chaplain (4160)

Life of St. Meriasek

120. A Feeble Man or a Cripple (4181)

Note: Numerals in brackets represent first line spoken.

First-line numerals in the text conform with those of W. Stokes' 1872 edition, even when I have added occasional lines and have dispensed with others for the sake of consistency of translation. Thus, it should prove an easy matter to cross-reference with the Cornish text.

Readers please note:
These lines are for shouting across an open-air round theatre in the Medieval Theatre style.

FIRST DAY OF THE PLAY

DIAGRAM OF ROUND THEATRE

Heaven

Torturers   Silvester

Hell

                       Master

Bishop of Apollo

Outlaws   Bishop of Cornouailles

               Chapel

Count Rohan

                     Duke of Brittany ie

Duke of Cornwall   Father of Meriasek

Emperor Teudar   King Conan

              Constantine

THE LIFE OF ST. MERIASEK

Here begins the play of the Life of Saint Meriasek, Bishop and Confessor

Meriasek's Father shall parade here

Meriasek's Father
1. I am the Duke of Brittany,
   Raised up from royal blood,
   Chieftain of all this country,
   Next to the high and good
   King Conany.
   Of his lineage I am,
   Master over wild and tame:
   The Lords all fear me greatly.

9. Actually, one son we have,
   Meriasek by name.
   Now I'll put the little knave
   To school, to learn the game
   Of goodness. If it be God's will,
   I'd like to elevate him
   To great excellence — until
   Ruler of kingdoms he become.

Meriasek's Mother
17. My Lord, it's a good thing
    To raise him up on high.
    Now he reads well, he can bring
    His mind to grammar, and apply
    Himself meetly.
    I was just remarking
    To your Father — are you looking
    Forward to school, my sweety?

Meriasek

25. Oh parents, all my training
Is studying and learning.
For, just to know the Scripture,
Distinguish good and evil,
If I could, of truth, gain that skill,
It would be all my pleasure.

Meriasek's Father

31. Meriasek, God's blessing!
Always a good heart you bring:
Of goodness a ripe scholar.
Messenger, off with you — away —
And my dearest son convey
Unto the Grammar Master.

First Messenger

38. It shall be as my Lord says.
I know precisely the part
Where the Grammar Master stays.
He has a generous heart
For these most dear little boys.
Meriasek, when you're ready,
We'll leave at a steady
Pace on the road to this same place.

Meriasek

45. Oh Father and Mother mine,
Your blessings I beseech you,
That I may learn in my time,
Ever more grace and goodness too:
For, your blessings
Are a far greater treasure
Than wealth of any measure,
Or any worldly trappings.

Meriasek's Father

53. Sweet son, God's blessing to thee
    And my blessing forever.
    As long as I live, I shall see
    That purpose of yours fails never.
    Well now, Squire,
    Off you go with my son.
    Take care of the little one,
    Perchance there of goodness learn:
    If of such thy mind take fire.

Meriasek's Mother

62. My son, may Mary bless thee,
    And now, let me caress thee
    With a kiss — for I assess
    That only true tenderness
    Is fitting, Meriasek.
    I trust God in his firmament,
    When parents are infirm and spent,
    Our good orders you'll not neglect.

The Duke's Squire

70. Meriasek, let's depart.
    Not a glimmer of the art
    Of writing's yet come my way.
    No: I don't know a letter,
    Still, I pray for something better.
    God *us* speed — that's all I say.

Master

76. I am a master of grammar,
    Graduate of Bonnilapper —
    A university somewhat small.
    I'm a dab hand at quotation,
    And after imbibition,
    I speak just Latin, you know.

First Messenger

82. Honour to you, Grammar Master,
And always great renown.
Education's what we're after,
And this is Duke Conan's son.
He has been sent
To you for his instruction.
Teach him with your good unction:
Duke Conan will pay the rent.

Master

90. Messenger, have not a fear.
He will get such teaching here
To surpass all grammar scholars.
Meriasek, sit down where
The other boys are sitting there,
And look at your primers —
Or say a recitation.
There'll be some elapsation
Whilst a poor master recovers.

First Scholar

99. God help A B C —
The end of the verse is D.
I don't know any more
In the book. I didn't arrive
At school until nightfall
Yesterday. But I will strive
When I've seen the dining hall.

Second Scholar

106. E S T — that is "est."
I don't know quite what comes next.
Oh dear Master, please don't beat
Me. I'll be so much better,
Know my verses to the letter,
Once I've had something to eat.

Master

112. Well — go and learn with thy kind,
And when you want, go and dine.
Meriasek, go with like mind,
For in age you're but a sweeting,
And young children all love eating:
Thus my living I must find.

Meriasek

118. I tell you, my Master,
So you won't be made angry,
I intend to fast, for
Today it is Friday.
It's good to think of the soul,
And the Passion of our Lord,
Which for us, Jesus bore.
I'll fast this meal-time — that's all.

126. And every Friday which comes 'round,
Throughout the whole long year.
To Heav'n I shall make my sound,
Not eat nor drink my beer.

130. I'll go to the chapel good,
To Christ who shed his own blood,
To offer up my prayer;
And to Mary his mother,
Before food or any other,
I shall pray, as always, there.

Master

136. Oh my son, do as you wish,
For I see you're meant for bliss.
Meriasek, now I know —
So come and go as you please.
We'll do all we can to ease
Your duties, yes, as from now.

He goes down alone to the chapel

Meriasek *(in the chapel)*

142. Jesu of earth and Heaven Lord,
To thee I make my prayer.
Jesu, of thee I do implore,
Against temptation make me beware.
Jesu, keep me in accord
All my days to serve thee fair.
Jesu, my strength and my word,
Body, spirit, without care,
I give to worship thee;
That I may, humble and meek,
Never look for, never seek
The lust the world will offer me.

154. Mary, Queen of Heaven free,
Mother, most holy seeming,
Mary, raise, in charity,
Thy hand, to the child of learning.
Mary, Mother, pray for me,
That the Devil never bring
Upon me his might,
Nor my enemy his brother
World, nor Flesh, nor any other:
My heart I'll make contrite.

164. And so, while I watch and pray,
I shall wish
To please Christ,
From youth to my dying day.

He goes off to the Master

King Conan parades

King Conan

168. I am called Conany,
Of Little Britain king.
Yes: I rule all Brittany.
I am their Sovereign.

Now, with all my meyny,
I'll visit my next of kin.
He's my head of Chivalry:
I trust that the Duke is in.
Here's the reason why:
For Meriasek, marriage!
They say amongst the peerage
That the girl's parentage
Is unequalled 'neath the sky.

First Lord
181. He's a very prudent child,
Polite, modest and mild
Above children of his kind:
And may I say, supreme Lord,
He'd suit an empress, on my word —
If there were any to find.

Second Lord of the King
187. Meriasek's loved by all,
Amongst the great and the small,
For the good that he employs.
And indeed, I have to tell
You that there's no equal
For saintliness in other boys.

Meriasek
193. I pray you, my dear master,
Would you be so kind
As to let me see my Father,
And the Mother I left behind?
Please say that you won't mind.
Oh thankyou for my schooling.
To the Masters, my blessing.
You've taught me well, they'll find.

Master
201. My boy, Christ's blessing to you,
And my own blessing too.

Now thou art truly blessed!
Never was there in my school
A boy with learning such as you,
Nor full of such true goodness.

Meriasek goes down with the Squire
and returns to his father

Meriasek

207. Joy to my worthy father,
And my reverence always.
True joy to my dear mother,
Goodness, honour all your days.
I have such a tale to tell!
Please give to me your blessing.
Now I have complete learning,
With the Holy Ghost's sending,
And Christ, Lord of the angels.

Father

216. Meriasek, welcome home,
And my full blessing to thee.
If full of learning thou hast come,
And not of stupidity,
Then I am pleased indeed.
Knights, you'd better make ready.
A visitor — King Conany —
Comes here tonight, at great speed.

Mother

224. My son, Christ's blessing to thee,
And thy Mother's blessing too.
Thou art worthy, as I see,
For the good that thou dost do.
We've been told all about
How good at school, and free
You've been, with generosity.
All Brittany knows: no doubt!

King Conan *(to the Duke)*

232. Reverence, worthy Sir Duke —
A body of some power.
I have come tonight to look
At matters concerning our
Family good.
Joy to you, gracious Lady,
And that dear son who's with thee,
Meriasek, my own blood.

Meriasek's Father

240. Welcome, liege, we're glad you've come,
You are welcome to our home,
You and all your people.
We're so happy you are here,
We'll be gladder a whole year,
For seeing you in our castle.

Meriasek's Mother

246. You are welcome, our Lord King,
For great happiness you bring,
So pleased to see you are we.
More welcome a man never
Will receive in this house, ever;
Even my father who reared me.

Meriasek

252. Welcome to this place, liege royal,
Our head and principal,
Above us all entirely.
You are worthy of revering
Because of your good ruling.
Great and small, governed are we.

King Conan

258. Great thanks. Before we disperse,
I should like us to converse
About a good and worthy thing.

My son, I'd like to propose,
Without seeming to impose
On our blood, the youngest spring . . .

Meriasek's Father, the Duke

264. Well, let us first go to eat.
Everyone into the palace.
Great and small shall find a seat.
Spencer — are you sure there's space?
Spencer — are we going to greet
Them with a table of grace?
Oh dear — tell me that it's fit
For the dining of His Grace.

all go down to the Plain

The Duke of Brittany's Spencer

272. Everything here is ready.
Let the Lords be seated by
You, Meriasek, my lord.
So, now we'll bring in the food.
Blow, trumpets, clarions good!
Merriment, upon my word!

Meriasek

278. Please take your seat here, your grace.
Yours is the rightful first place.
Now, facing you, my Father,
And dear Mother at the head.
Now, Orleans, Duke of dread
Power, sit at this other —
And the lords, young or grey-haired,
Some here, some there, no bother.

Duke of Orleans

286. Thankyou, Meriasek, lad.
Your rearing — opposite of bad —
Has endeared you to many;

And your manners too have had
Good effect on layman and letterêd.
Your like in this world — there aren't any!

Meriasek

292. My liege lord, be you merry,
You and all the company,
Dukes, Earles, Knights, parents who took part
In my rearing; my Father
Rest yourself, and Mother,
With all my heart.

King Conan

298. Meriasek, I thank thee.
I find thee so courteous,
A powerful man I'll make thee.
I think I know — without fuss —
Where a match with a worthy
King's daughter — fortuitous
In the matter of dowry
Might be made — for with her must
Come manors, towns, you see,
Villages: well, shall I just
Say who she is to the company?[1]

Meriasek's Father, the Duke

308. Great thanks to our good liege.
We shall always acknowledge
Our thanks for your good intention.
To us strength would be added
If he were to be married
Well: bounty, not to mention.

---

[1]An extra line has been added to the verse to retain the pace and flow of the speech in the exposition of the King's thoughts. In the Cornish, the verse has 10 lines of ABABABABAB.

Please note: throughout this translation, such discrepancies occur. Line numbering is based on W. Stokes' edition, to facilitate cross-referencing with the Cornish text.

Mother

314. We are very pleased to be
Guided by you, certainly,
And Meriasek too,
Or on ourselves blame to shed.
Of our family you're the head,
Liege governor of grace true.

Meriasek

320. My liege lord, much thanks to you
For all your good intention.
So you should not take it ill,
Before all let me mention,
Without dissention:
Forgive me, parents, I will
Not give myself up to
The world, nor any union.

Father

328. Meriasek, be quiet.
Thou shalt get thee married yet
To some good worthy lady;
And we shall be the stronger
Through this marriage, forever —
And all thy line, certainly.

Mother

334. If he doesn't get married,
We'll be mocked and chided.
Meriasek don't be foolish.
You've gained a reputation
In the world for your wisdom.
For shame, let thy good name flourish.

Meriasek

340. For all the world, don't speak a word
Ever of marriage to me.
My mind is set upon a road,
Which yet you cannot see.

Father
344. What road? What road is that, son?
Meriasek, you tell me.
I hope you're not having fun
With us — 'twould be a pity.

Meriasek
348. By the grace of Lord Jesus,
My dear father, I will not.
To worship Christ, my wish is
To be made a knight of God,
Of the order that pleases
Me: and thus consecrated,
Live in thankful gladness
Throughout life's span allotted.

King Conan
356. What need hast thou to renounce
The gifts the world will bring you —
And of your blood, every ounce,
Father's and Mother's side, true blue!
My son, this is not respect
For thine own good family.
And I beg, most earnestly,
Let other roads thy mind project.

Father
363. Meriasek, it's a shame
Thou wast ever sent to school.
I don't know where I'm to blame.
With sorrow my heart is full.
And as for knowledge —
Thou showest not a small trace.
We'll not be able to face
The people. Then there's the case
Of the estate and no marriage . . .

Meriasek

372. Oh father, make Christ your heir,
Or give it to the next in line:
Lands, farms, whatever, I don't care.
For meddling I've got no time.

King Conan

376. Meriasek, I advise
You, it is not over wise
To act against a parent.
I just don't know what clap-trap
You learnt at school — there's no scrap
Of goodness in you — that's patent!

Meriasek

382. Christ says: whosoever
Would wish to follow me,
Let him forsake father,
Mother, friends and family;
And all of his land,
All of his towns, small and great,
Let him all of them forsake:
A hundred gifts then shall he take,
And dwell amongst the heavenly band.
All this, without exception,
According to St. Luke.
I'll find the passage mentioned
In his gospel, in the Book.

King Conan

395. Why can't you just get married
Here on earth like other men?
Many worthies have carried
Duty and love of God to the end.
By all the saints in Heaven,
I am most displeased with thee,
For causing so much worry.
Well, we'll bear their mockery, then.

Meriasek

403. For Christ's Heavenly love,
I beg you, don't suffer grief
Just on my account, nor move
To sorrow, for my belief.

King Conan

407. Now listen, Meriasek,
In fairness I request thee,
Or else thou wilt regret it,
I say to thee most frankly —
Consider well.
Thy father and I, we can,
If we please, convey the land
To some entirely different man;
Then come to thee it never shall.

416. As a beggar wilt thou be
Considered, indubitably,
Throughout the land.
And all thy kin will be blamed.
Alas if we should be shamed.
Let some better ways be planned.

Meriasek

422. If another estate can be
Made out of it, most certainly,
My gentle liege, I'm delighted.
That will give me no worry.
If I have Heaven's country,
Fie to the world's pleasures blighted.

King Conan

428. I marvel you fie and blight
All the riches of the world,
When you would not see the light
Of day for long — nor any churl —

Without wealth and the good right
Of chivalry. Amongst earls
Or lords received a man might
Be, and always honoured.

436. Through his wealth, a royal man made,
Aways placed in the high grade.
But what is the poor man worth?
Though his ancestry be great,
Outside, with uncovered pate,
Noticed by no-one of Birth.

Meriasek
442. Do not talk of chivalry.
No more are riches my concern.
Many are deluded, I see,
By the world's wealth; nor learn

446. From Dives, who was wealthy
Enough, at all seasons.
Whither went his soul, think ye?
To Hell! To the fiends! Reasons

450. Enough? But we also read
Of Lazarus — poor indeed —
Who bore hard labour sweetly.
When he was dead, Abraham
Took him in his own bosom,
And kept him in glory.

King Conan
456. Sirs, get up from the table.
I'm sorry that I came here.
Wretched man — are you unable
To see any sense? Do you fear
That a rich man can never
Go to the good Heaven? By Gad,
I think you've gone crackers, mad
And potty, by my soul here.

Meriasek

464. A rich man is as able
To go to Heaven, says the scripture,
As is a ship's great cable
Through a needle's aperture.
Thus is a rich man's labour.

469. But this, by unravelling,
Can be helped, by undoing.
The rich man should take warning
His wealth to be distributing,
In charity, to the poor.

King Conan

474. Sir Duke, goodbye.
By Christ, my guide,
Thy son is mad.
Through him, I fear,
My journey here
Has gone to bad;
And my labouring.
Let me tell him,
I shan't like him,
As long as I am living.

Conan goes off

Father

484. Very great thanks to you, Lord,
For showing him charity.
Sadly, *you'll* get *your* reward
If you won't, through propriety,
Be guided.
The prince of this country is
Displeased with thee — yes he is —
And thy parents chided.

Meriasek

492. Though you are displeased with me,
It is all against my will.
With Jesus Christ of mercy
I am in agreement still.
Father and Mother, give me
Your own dear blessings until
I go — immediately —
To learn of goodness my fill.
For love of the Trinity,
Do not tempt me to do ill.

Father

502. Into the hands of God on high,
My son, I shall entrust thee.
"Yours to know the reason why,"
And my blessing upon thee.
I cannot do any more.

Mother

507. Amen too, and thee I bless.
My son, give to me thy kiss.
Very sad am I at this,
At parting forever more.

Here Meriasek wears a priest's gown

Here the Bishop of Cornouailles shall parade

Bishop

511. I am a bishop in Brittany,
In a province called Cornouailles.
There are few equals to me,
Being full of grace and all wise.
I am a prelate so proud,
A prince over the clerics.
There are not in these districts
My equals: give that no doubt!

Meriasek

519. Sir Bishop, much joy to you!
And now I do beseech you
To grant me holy orders.
To be a priest, I would show
Joy, administering to
The people Christ's body. Oh,
I'll hope to please examiners.

The Bishop of Cornouailles goes down into the 'place"

The Bishop of Cornouailles

526. Dear Meriasek, welcome.
My dear son, I have heard some
Good things spoken about thee.
Of course you shall be ordained,
Right away, in Jesus' name.
Ordained by me. Certainly!

he kneels

May Christ always maintain
Thee ever in purity.

Blind Man

534. God's blessing, good people.
I'm a blind man, unable
To see. Do me some favour
With alms, and I'll pray for you
To merciful Christ Jesu,
The Christians' own dear Saviour.

Cripple

540. I too am much disabled.
My limbs are bunched and crippled,
Rotten. Scarcely can I start
To try to think of walking.
I ask succour and healing
From you, sir, with all my heart.

¹i.e. to the Round, from his scaffold.

Meriasek
546. Lord Jesus, I pray to thee,
Cure this man who has no sight.
Jesus Christ in Majesty,
Heal this blind man with thy might.
Lord Jesus, so full of grace,
Heal likewise this other wight.
Jesus, royal supremacy
Display, a virgin's son hight.
Heal this man now.
In nomine Patris et Filii,
May the power of Christ heal thee,
From this moment, be made whole.

Blind Man
558. May Christ Jesu repay thee!
For now, very well I see!
I know that thy prayer is blessed,
I know it; and certainly,
Ever glorious, thy words expressed.

Cripple
563. And I, who for years endured
This sore affliction, am cured.
In this world I'm cured, it's clear,
Of my sickness:
Thanks to Jesus,
And this man here.

he crosses into the 'place'

Bishop of Cornouailles
569. Meriasek, reverence!
Loved by God of deliverance,
I know truly that thou art.
Will you stay with me a while?
On thee I shall always smile,
And we won't part.

Meriasek

575. Sir Bishop, much thanks to you.
Now I have decided to
Go to another country.
Blessings of all the sainted
To you and your acquainted,
And all your company.

The Bishop of Cornouaille's Crozier-Bearer

581. Meriasek, God's blessing.
It would be very pleasing
To us, if you would remain.
But, not for us
To make a fuss,
Or to detain.

The Bishop of Cornouailles goes up

Meriasek

587. Sailors, accept a blessing.
If to Cornwall you're sailing,
I should like to go with you.
I haven't much to offer,
But I'll ask Christ to proffer
Largesses upon you too.

Sailor

593. Thou'rt welcome with us, good friend.
We will take thee to Lands End,
Through God's will 'fore the week's through.

he goes up into the ship

Come aboard here right away,
And, my sailors, no delay:
Hoist up the sail for me now.

Sailor's Servant
599. See — it's right up to the top.
Right now, mate, make fast the rope.
The wind is really blowing,
And the mad sea's being tossed.
I believe we'll all be lost,
And drowned here, where we're standing.

The Sailor
605. Pity we were ever born.
Altogether we'll be gone.
To each other let's confess
Now, there is no other way:
We won't see another day.
Sad to come to this distress!

Meriasek
611. Oh be ye of good comfort.
We are able to resort
To Christ, who will help all ye.
I'll ask him for His support,
Whether at sea or in port:
So you need not have a hurt
If you call on Christ and me.

Sailor
618. Meriasek, worshipped be thou!
Through thee are we saved, somehow,
From peril, and that's for sure.
Go thou ashore, O good man.
In Cornwall, thanks to Jesus, land,
According to thy wish now.

He disembarks in Cornwall

Meriasek
624. To Jesu be the glory.
I am in a strange country
Here, so I say.
I will go and walk ashore.

May the Dear Heart, Jesus Lord,
Guide me to a place to stay,
Worship to Him thus accord,
And to Mary, flower of maids.

632. I have come onto the land,
Mary, Mother and Maiden.
From walking, I can scarce stand.
If there's a house or mansion
Of thine near here,
Oh please guide me now to it,
For I would make a place fit
For an orat'ry, and commit
It to the name of Mary dear.
Joy to you, good man, where you sit!
What chapel is this one here?

Domestic Servant
643. Say no more: I will tell thee.
That same house is called Mary
Of Camborne's chapel.
Where are you from, to ask it?
Come on, now, you tell me that,
My good fellow.

Meriasek
649. I have come from Brittany
Over the sea to this country,
As God willed, for my teaching.
And by the chapel I'll make,
For the blessed Mary's sake,
An oratory building.
Is there any water here?
For no other drink — no fear —
Shall my mouth be opening.

Domestic Servant
658. Water is very scarce here.
It's necessary to bear

Off a long way to get it.
If I could get ale or wine,
I wouldn't drink water, mind,
'Twouldn't be for my benefit.

Meriasek

664.   I'll go and wander around.
Perhaps water can be found,
North-east of the chapel here.

he crosses to the meadow

667.   Jesu, Lord, I pray to thee,
Jesu, grant water to me,
Jesu, through thy grace, quickly,
As Moses, previously,
From the hard scree.

here the well springs up water

Domestic Servant

672.   Oh, good man, you should be blessed
For bringing relief to us,
Such good, clear and sweet water.
Here it is openly proved
Before us, that you are loved
By Him, our God, the Father.

Fever-Patient

678.   Oh God, alas, is there aught
Now? The "thief disease" I've caught —
The disease called "the season."
I have had the runs for months,
The pain not subsided once;
My heart and bowels are all wan!

Cripple

684.   I'm malformed, don't be misled.
God! I wish that I were dead
And gone from this bad old world.

There is living in Camborne
A man able to perform
Quiet miracles, I'm told.
Better go this very morn
And pray for a cure, out bold.

they go over to Meriasek

Fever-Patient
692. Meriasek, joy to thee.
We are two poor men, you see.
I'm suffering from fever,
And this man with me is maimed.
To tell the truth, I'm ashamed:
Can't earn our living, either
One. Cure us, in Jesus' name.
From our sickness, make us free.

Meriasek
700. Jesu, Lord of Heaven and earth,
Grant, by his grace, health to you.
Jesu, I pray with all my worth,
Now heal both these men anew.
Mary, Mother above earth,
Pray to thy Son for these two.
Mary of the Virgin birth,
Pray for me, and help me through.
Stand up, good men, and come forth.
Tell me — how do you feel now?

Cripple
710. Oh worship Christ here revealed!
Legs and body all are healed.
I can walk without complaint.

Fever-Patient
713. Thanks to Christ, I have my cure.
To Meriasek, the pure,
God's fortune, it does not fail.
To worship him we are bound,
Even if danger prevail.

Meriasek

718. Give your thanks to Christ, good men,
Attribute nothing to me.
Here now, a place I intend
To found, through Christ of Mercy.
This will I do.
In honour of this event,
For worship, any moment,
A church I'll build, that's my intent,
Beside Mary's chapel, too.

A Sick Man

727. Oh, alas, what shall I do?
Here on my face fell a too
Awful disease. No-one wants
To look at me. But I've heard
There's a Camborne doctor, by word
Of mouth, healing folk. There's a chance,
If I left now, and I cared
To see him, I might be cured.

735. Meriasek, joy to thee.
I'm a poor man, as you see.
For Christ's sake, give me your aid.
On my face is a disease;
It makes people ill at ease.
No-one sees me: they're afraid.

Meriasek

741. Oh help thee, Lord of Heaven!
Before this, He cured Naaman
Of this disease, leprosy.
Now I wash thee with water.
Jesus, Merciful Father,
If the hour has come, cure thee.

Domestic Servant

747. Well might you be joyful, mate.
You've been healed, and no mistake.

Thanks to Meriasek say,
For he is right filled with grace,
And loved too by God of grace,
As we see, lettered and lay.

Sick Man
753. Meriasek, thanks to you.
I beseech Christ, of grace full,
To repay you in Heaven.
And the glorious Virgin Mary.
There are many, so I see,
Healed by you, of this world's men.

let him go off

Here Meriasek waits at Camborne

Here Teudar shall parade

759. Well now — Teudar is my name,
Reigning Lord in Cornwall.
That Mahound gets holy fame
Is my charge, without fail,
Both far and near.
Whoever worships any
Other God shall have many
Pains: and a cruel death, I fear.

Messenger
767. Hail to you, Sir Lord Teudar.
I have brought with me some news.
But there are somewhat fewer
Things I'd tell you, could I choose.
I hardly dare —
For well I know,
Upon my soul,
You won't me spare.

Teudar

775. What has happened? At the nones!
Come on, tell me, you sluggard,
Speak! You false-tongued bag of bones!
Doesn't he hear? Cloth-eared bugger.
Speak, you deaf man. Speak at once!
Aye! Do your throat a mischief.
Come on — speak, accursed son!
May the devil be your grief!

Messenger

783. There's a priest here, so they say,
In Penwith, doing his work,
Just a bit west of Carn Brea.
He's been healing the blind folk,
The deaf and maimed,
Every disease in the world.
Anyway, that's what I've heard.
He won't have a god named
But only that of Christ who died,
And when He was dead, became
Raised to life there, where He lied.

Teudar

793. Oh! Woe is me for sorrow!
Where shall I find a devil's tomb?
Pity I couldn't borrow
Death before my mother's womb
Rejected me. Woe, for shame!
Soldiers! Soldiers, will you come,
So that we can soon do some
Settling up, in the devil's name.

First Soldier

801. My Lord, we will go with you.
I heard about that man too.
I've known about him for months.

He heals the blind — that is true,
Also, there are quite a few
With hearing who were deaf once.

Second Soldier

807. I tell you, my Lord Teudar,
That this very intruder
Has the country all agog.
If he can't be persuaded
To change his mind, downgraded
Will be Mahound, like a dog.

Teudar *descends*

813. I've heard enough.
Come! Let's be off.
We'll march, my knights.
You there! Tell me,
Just where is he?
We'll put this right!

Messenger

819. Royal Lord, I see
Him certainly,
There, in the plain,
Coming, I tell you,
From the chapel.
There he is again!

Teudar

825. Hey you! Bachelor! Over here!
Tell me your name quick, my dear,
Also your creed.
I'd like to hear
With my own ear
Also, what's your breed.

Meriasek

831. Meriasek is my name,
Raised from blood of Conan's line.
I believe in Christ, who came

From Heaven to save us in time.
Christ, God indeed,
Born of Mary, his mother;
She, a maiden, no other:
That I know. That is my creed.

Teudar
839. Thou art raised of worthy blood,
Meriasek: be advised.
Do not talk of things that could
Not have been witnessed, nor lies:
No, I tell you.
It is against all reason
That a child, any season,
Could be conceived — no my eyes! —
Without some man's seed there too!

Meriasek
848. Ah! Thou dost not understand
The law quite as thou shouldst do,
Of the glorious Birth and
The Passion of Jesus too.
Here on this earth,
The sun shines, and the glass will stand
The rays passing through — thus planned
God above; and by his hand
The Holy Spirit was manned.
He was conceived, and his birth
Like the clear glass, made of sand,
Witnesses its truth and worth.

Teudar
860. Don't you bandy words with me,
Though you yap forever — see?
Now, Jesus had a father,
As he had a mother too.
What you say is just not true.
It's all a load of pother.

Meriasek

866. Of course God was his Father,
If you could understand it.
He came to save the childer.
Of Adam, as He planned it.
For this, his death was cruel,
Mankind was in Satan's grip:
But he saved all mankind's soul,
Brought them to bliss from the pit.

Teudar

874. Now Meriasek, I say,
If God was his Father
Above, then by his grace,
He could have saved all other,
Both rich and poor,
Without being killed here.
Shameful is this account of yours.
Why slay God's Son like a deer?

Meriasek

882. Through Adam our father's sin,
Damned was he and all his sons,
But the Godhead desired him
To be redeemed again at once
To salvation.
And so, conceived was the Son.
He took manhood to him,
For the Godhead could not come
To suffer Passion.

Teudar

891. No good will come of arguing,
Though we were here forever.
Meriasek, Christ denying,
Our friendship I won't sever.
A great bishop

I'll make thee, you then being
Pre-eminent ruler. Nothing
Do I ask, nothing
But that Mahound you worship.

Meriasek
900. There is a much better way:
You worship dear Christ alway,
Otherwise you're surely lost.

Teudar
903. Don't argue one word of Christ.
Listen to me and be wise,
Or it'll be to your cost,
Because when I have a fit,
The Devil out of his pit
Will come, before I'm crossed.

909. Well, dear Meri-
asek, sorry
To do you ill.
Worship lovely
Gods of mine. See
Then how you feel.

Meriasek
915. Certainly devils are thy
Gods, so three thousand times fie
On them. Do not look to me
For pity. Deny them if thou
Wishest to be a good man now.
Foolish to trust them: you'll see.

Teudar
921. Away with thee, conjurer,
For disavowing prime gods.
Thou shalt hang on the clapper's
Gallows for the just rewards
Of your prince and emperor.

Come here, thou fool!
I shall always detest thee
The more, fled from thy country
An outlaw. Speak against me
And thou'lt bewail.

930. I am Emperor
And Governor,
Conqueror of land,
An honoured lord.
Great is my word.
Know I am grand.

Meriasek
936. Silence! Hold thine idle chatter.
Thy wind makes too much clatter
Here. Now — without any lies,
Better for thee to be Christian,
Wholeheartedly, in my opinion.
So now, thee I will baptize.

Teudar
942. Ah! Help! Get out of the way!
Oh! Woe is me, I must run.
The Devil's come here, I say,
And wants to baptize me. One
Minute more in this playing-
Place and my death has begun.
Mahound! Show thyself today
To that man, and have some fun.

he goes up

950. Tormentors, into the playing-
Place! Tormentors, here, I say!
If you're with us, come at once.
Oh? Don't trouble yourselves, my dear!
We'll have to fetch them, I fear.
Teudar himself has to hunt.

he goes down

Sticks ready for Teudar and his men

956. How now! Where are ye, my mates?
Curses on your skulls and pates!
What are you about? Napping?
Didn't you here my lamentation?
Here! A friendly little donation
For you. Go on! Start thrashing!

and they shall beat them

First Torturer

962. Sir Lord, don't thrash us any more,
But tell us what you need.
We'll do it all at speed.

Teudar

965. Go to Camborne for me —
West of Carn Brea — quickly.
There, you'll find a defiant
Chap. He is undoubtedly
A Devil: rely on it.

970. Meriasek is his name,
And he believes in Christ.
When you see him, seize this same
Man and torment him — be nice.
If he won't deny Christ's fame,
Cuse the bastard — be precise.
If you kill him, I shan't blame
You; I'll uphold you in a trice.

Second Torturer

978. Lord, we will do that for you,
And be off without more ado.
Let each from his quarter spy.
By my soul, I shall guide you
To Camborne. Now we must fly!

Meriasek

983. Oh, great thanks be to the Lord!
By a vision I am warned
That I should leave this country
And go right away, abroad,
Now, quickly to Brittany.
There, Teudar I shall avoid.
His plot will fail certainly.

990. Here have I founded a mansion
By Mary of Camborne's side.
Jesus Christ, thy devotion
Bestow on this house, every tide,
So that, from this time, attention
And honour be given, far and wide.
Also to Mary,
The Trinity of the Father,
The seven sacraments, whether
On work or feast days fairly.

1000. Should a faithful Christian
Fall ill from "the season,"
And remember me here,
Lord Jesus, with reason,
Will then save him: no fear.

1005. Likewise, I pray that the fountain
Will be a cure, for certain,
For a man who is deranged.
Jesus, Lord of Salvation,
Grant this by benediction,
And let such a man be changed.

1011. My blessing with thee, O place
And mansion. In a short space
Of time I must leave thee. Near
Are my enemies. I will
Keep to the downs, and rest still
Now, under the rock that's here.

*Here Meriasek
hides under the rock*

53

Second Torturer

1017.   Have you seen Meriasek?
That sharp-eyed fellow — Oh heck!
I'm sure he's not in Camborne.

Third Torturer

1020.   May you never get your supper!
And may he come a cropper
On his mother's curse — he's gorn!

A Menial

1023.   Look in the bushes and at
The rock too, in case he's sat
Down, hiding here on the ground . . .
Leave him! Let's go home. No matter.
He doesn't want to be found.

First Torturer

1028.   What devil's hole has he gone
Into? Teudar will go bonkers
When he hears he has escaped.

Second Torturer

1031.   That's his fault. He should have done
His thing before. He could have won
His argument where his mouth gaped.

Third Torturer

1034.   Hail, Teudar in thy tower!
I can tell thee this hour
That Meriasek is fled.
That's all we know. In town and
Downs — nowhere in the land.
Of him, no more can be said.

Teudar

1040.   Oh! Oh woe! Oh! Oh!
If he has fled the country!
I wouldn't want that — no —

Not for a share of money
Equal to twice the lolly
In all the world. No! Oh no!
Oh! You drunken sots! I'll go
And cry on you eternally.

Menial

1048. Aye, Teudar, go on! Go wrong!
God's curse on thy mother's son.
You were busy parlying.
Pardon me, but I'm thinking
His God looks after him, again.

Teudar

1054. Is this all the comfort I
Am going to get from you?
Oh Sirs, this is all sport, by
Your thinking, while I grieve too.
Well! Never mind!
By Apollo, my glorious God,
Before we part, only one sod
Or two will be laughing. Kind
Payment I will make to the
Hobbyhorse and his cronies.
Take that! Four useless phonies.
Next time, remember orders — huh?

Meriasek

1065. Thanks be to Jesus alone.
I've rested under this stone,
My enemies departed.
They could never get to me:
God willed it so, this I see,
God, the very great-hearted.
I name this rock, before we're parted,
Meriasek's Rock. Let's get started.

1074. I will stay close by the sea,
To try and find a passage.
God bless you, good Master free,
And keep your ship from ravage.
If you be bound
For Brittany, then I would
Beg to go — that's if you could
Arrange that a space be found.

Shipmaster
1082. You would seem an honest man.
Come, in God the Father's name.
Come aboard with us, now.
Hoist up the sail, mate. The wind
Is fair. Cornwall is behind
Us, Brittany at the bow.

Crewman
1088. The Channel is safely crossed.
We got here with no time lost.
That was quite good going.
So, now that we have made land,
Go ashore, it's right at hand,
No need for any rowing.
Even the rock has bowed down
To welcome thee to this ground!
And that is Jesus' doing.

Meriasek
1097. Good man, may God repay you.
Now, full of grace Lord Jesu,
Guide me onto the best way.
If I go to my kinsmen,
I'll be tempted, this I ken,
By all the lusts of the day.

A Breton

1103. Good man, take care where you go.
There is a wolf on that road,
A great big one.
If he comes near you, you will
Find he will make your blood spill.
For, that he's already done.

Meriasek

1109. Beast, I command you to do
No mischief to me, nor to
Any Christian — not ever.
Have no fear at all, good man,
He will let me take him, and
Handle him. Altogether
Like a gentle little lamb
Following. No violence, either.

Breton

1117. You are surely a blessed man.
He has continually slain,
Many men and children too,
In this country. We are greatly
Obliged, good man. How gently,
Like a lamb, he follows you.

Meriasek

1123. He did not offer violence,
Nor shall he receive injury.
Beast, in the name of Christ, hence
To the wilderness, I tell thee.
Do not interfere
With any man's son from this
Day. For Jesus' sake in bliss,
Go thy ways, no more amiss.
Don't linger here.

1132. To the wilderness I go,
       To be a hermit, and so
       Worship my God properly.
       No temptation,
       Degradation,
       Or things worldly.

1138. Indeed, here by the castle
       Called Pontivy, on the hill,
       By Josselin river will nestle
       A chapel, which build I will,
       For Mary,
       Where she may be worshipped freely,
       Though the place be hard and rocky,
       And the climate be chilly.

he goes up the mountain

1146. Glory to Christ, Virgin's Son.
       A thousand paces the mountain
       Is from the ground. I know the one
       God will help me.
       I will establish
       My own house forthwith,
       With foundations, as you see.

A chapel ready.
Here he wears a russet mantle and a beard

THE LIFE OF SILVESTER

Here begins the Life of St. Silvester

Constantine *shall parade here saying:*

1153. Because I am a person
Without peer and quite dreaded,
My name could be only one —
Constantine the noble. Head
Of the country, Emperor,
Son to the Queen Helena,
Head of all this area,
As everyone knew before.

1161. There is, in this our country,
A false belief now current,
Making me very angry.
Before my life is spent,
I shall tame it, yes, you'll see.
I shall stop it, as I meant
To before. I've killed many
Already, with quite stringent
Punishments, and I'll do more.
Torturers! They're crazy folks.
Torturers! They're all mad blokes.
Do Mahound and Sol a favour.

Here the torturers shall parade with swords

1172. Hail Constantine the noble!
As we are thy loyal people,
We have come all together
To worship and honour thee.
If we get your enemy,
They won't be showing much glee.

59

Constantine

1178. Welcome, you knights, everyone!
I want you all to proceed
To chastise Christians — have fun —
All over Rome. Now take heed —

1182. All who believe in Mary's Son,
Go and slay them in torment.
Never fear any damnation:
I'll support you — that's my intent.

Second Torturer

1186. We fear not sin nor peril.
My arms are itching for the thrill.
I've been resting far too long,
Without murdering Christians.
Give orders to your partizans.
Standing around is all wrong.

Emperor Constantine

1192. Some armed men shall go with you,
About a hundred or two.
Try to prove yourselves manly.
Do not spare the young or grey
In spilling Christian blood, I say,
Enemies of Sol and me.

Third Torturer

1198. No, we shall not, Constantine.
They shall have a torment fine,
Who worship Christ the beggar.
Let's go right away, comrades!
Let us see if there parades
Any Christian traitor.

Menial

1204. There are two blokes over there.
Look. I see by their manner,
They would seem to be Christians.

Well, tell us now please, good sirs,
What you believe in, masters,
Otherwise you'll die with pains.

The Earl

1210. In Christ Jesus we believe,
And his name we will not leave
For fear of any man on earth.
Whoever believes not this
Shall go to Hell and not to bliss,
And nothing shall he be worth.

First Torturer

1216. Out upon thee, thou foul dog!
Do not name your Christ, that hog,
And if you do, you'll be dead.
We are sent by Constantine
To destroy the Christians.
Let it be known what I've said.

A Doctor in the Christian Faith

1122. Well, for fear of Constantine
Or torturers any time,
We would not deny Jesus.
If you should do anything
Against us, Christ, who is king
Over lords forgives the callous.

Second Torturer

1228. Thou whoreson, don't insult us.
Fie upon thee and on Christ.
Deny his name right away.
Worship Jove and Sol the famous,
Or you'll die of rigorous
Pains, friend, that's all I can say.

The Earl

1234. Better for us, then, to die,
Than worship in security

A Devil called Apollo.
Oh God, how foolish you are
Not to worship Christ. He bore
Cruel death for us all, you know.

Third Torturer
1240. For talking like a villain
You shall now go to prison,
And there you shall be strung up;
Also, the traitor with you.
He'll be at your side there too.
You'll be hanged, you cheeky pup.

Doctor in the Faith
1246. Oh Mary, Queen of Heaven,
Mary, for our Salvation
Pray, especially for our soul.
Oh you accursed people,
Think of your spirit feeble,
For fear of damnation foul.

A Menial
1252. Be quiet! Leave my redemption
To me. Have you heard mention
Of a soul left on this earth?
No. Though Heaven's gates be closed,
Hell's will be wide open, 'spose.
I don't care where I go forth.

The Earl
1258. Jesu, Lord of our nation,
Jesu, grant us salvation,
For we must needs to die here.
Oh blessed be this our time.
To thee my spirit I consign
And commend without any fear.

First Torturer

1264. Now they are on the gallows,
Let's give them a good few blows.
Let's run them through with our swords,
From one side to the other.
So let the devil bother.
This one is dead, mark my words.

Second Torturer

1270. I'll run through the other one.
Standing quiet's not much fun.
I've put it right through his guts.
I'll slit him across the head,
So that all his brains will spread
Across the ground, down the ruts . . .

Third Torturer

1276. We are ready to do bad.
May he who is not, be had!
Look at them upon the ground.
Their bodies are all broken
Like a badger, or like men
All torn up by a greyhound.

The Menial

1282. Such a god-forsaken bunch
Will often brag like that − punch
A broken man; but evil
Will fall upon you in time.
I'll say farewell. God's sublime
Curse on the company. 'Till then.

The Menial goes off and the Torturers
wait in the open

Jesus   *In Heaven saying*

1288. My angels, white as crystal,
The martyred souls — bring them all
Very very soon to joy.

For all their own temporal
Labour in the world shall fall
Happiness that shall not cloy.

Michael
1294.   Jesu, thy will shall be done.
Whoso are martyred — each one —
They shall all soon come to joy.
As we are commanded, begun
Is the task. It shall be done.

Gabriel
1300.   O thou very martyred souls,
Heaven's joy is granted whole
By dear Jesus Christ above.
Because of torment on earth
Done to your bodies, your worth
Is all Heaven's joy and love.

Here the souls ready

First Torturer
1306.   Oh oh dear friends, let's go quick.
Let's hide somewhere — that's the trick,
Or we'll all burn together.
Oh my dear life — now this light
Is fallen on us, so bright,
I'm startled and full of fear.

Here St. Silvester begins, saying:

St. Silvester
1312.   Peace to all, humble and meek.
In God's name, we do praise Him
Who made the world in a week,
By his two hands from the dim
Clay, the father of mankind.
Father, Son and Holy Ghost,

Three persons one Substance, Host.
That is the true faith, most
Of which the Church teaches, you'll find.

1321. Now together, my children,
Let us depart from this place,
To bury the good folk, then,
Who were martyred, through God's Grace,
By evil men.
The people of Constantine
The Christians to death consign
In this country — this I ken.

he goes down

The tomb ready

A Cardinal
1329. Silvester, our dear Father,
May Jesu, our own Saviour,
Always be here to help us.
Look — all the dead folk are here.
Put them in tombs from the bier,
And let's leave quickly — no fuss.

Here they bury them

Silvester
1335. Now that they are in the tomb,
May Jesus Christ now assume
Care of their souls. We shall go,
To try and keep far away
From Constantine now this day,
Or else by him, I dare say,
We shall soon be dead, I know.

1342. To the mountain Soracte
We must go — we cannot stay.
It's no good to stay in Rome.

Come with me, my disciples,
For a while, great and small, it is
Best to absent ourselves from home.

he goes up to Mount Soracte

A mask ready upon Constantine's face

Second Torturer *to Constantine*
1348. Hail, Sir, my lord Constantine.
We have, dead, some very fine
Christians — there's about three score,
Some hanged and some beheaded,
Some by horses' tails were led,
Some burnt in fire — a few more.

Let him go off

Constantine
1354. Oh, my good soldiers, go home,
The Devil look after you.
Sickness — leprosy has come
Upon me. I don't know how.
Alas, alas!
I have become a leper.
No-one now is a lover
Of my very ugly face.

Ah! Woe is me. What is best
For me now? What can I do?
Oh dear, I shall never rest
For taking an over-cruel
Attitude to Christians. Blest
Of joy I'll never be. Who
More than me wants to die lest
People saw and then withdrew?

Constantine the Leper

A Justice

1370. Let us send for the bishops,
And let the doctors come here.
They will tell us from their books
If in this world there's a cure
For the sickness.
They are very learned men.
Do not let any fear, then,
Trouble you. They cure disease.

Constantine

1378. Alright, Messenger, straightway
Bring the Bishop here to me,
And the great Doctor. They say
The best man of learning's he.
He knows it all.
Perhaps they can diagnose
What best to do. I suppose
We might have some strange windfall.

Second Messenger

1386. Hail, Emperor Constantine.
Here I am, and quite ready
To do what you now assign
To me. I'll not go slowly,
No, nor linger.
I shall fetch soon to your tower
The Bishop and the doctor.
In this I'll be no idler̄.

Here the Apollonian Bishop or the Doctor shall parade

Second Messenger

1394. Greetings, Bishop, in thy tower!
Greetings to you too, Doctor!
You are well met in one place.
To Constantine you must go.
Consider your answers now,
I'll tell you the problem, to save face.

1400. **Apollonian Bishop**
Welcome, speedy messenger.
Here already, on my soul!
What's up with Constantine, there?
Is he not completely whole?
Oh, do tell us.
If he is in some trouble,
We shall try to be helpful.
We can do that now: no fuss.

Doctor
1408. Blimey! Here's a good bargain.
Dear Messenger,
Tell me in your own good time,
Now the Emperor sublime —
What's happened to our master?

Second Messenger
1413. A segregated leper.
I have not seen on land nor
Sea a sight more sinister.

Doctor
1416. Aha! Oh yes, I knew it.
Carry under thine armpit,
Bachelor Jenkin, my book,
Which describes the best physic.
And praise me up — that's the trick.
I am a great doctor, look.

An earthen pot: the book ready, & the urinal inspected

Clerk Jenkin
1422. In easing constipation, sir,
Or stopping the tertian fever,
You do have a lot of luck.
But if you got a woman
By your side, you'd be proven
A very good man — no truck.   *he goes down to Constantine*

Apollonian Bishop

1428. Honour upon this, your see,
And joy to thee.
My dear lord of the Kingdom,
We have freely
With this trustee
Of yours, the messenger, come.

Constantine

1434. Welcome, sir, of bishops flower.
Welcome also, sir doctor.
Come on up, I do pray you.
You see my disease at once.
I can't conceal this grievance.
Can you offer me a cure?

Doctor

1440. I will look at your water,
And then, the dear Emperor
Shall have the answer to his case.

Justice

1443. I've already thought of this.
The urine's here, you'll notice.
Pour it into thy blue glass.

Doctor

1446. Hoc urum malorum,
Et nimis rubrorum.
Ah! I know very well.
Come here, Bachelor Jenkin.
Raise your face up — let's begin.
Come on, look up — bloody hell!

1452. Now, don't be distressed by it.
There's an odour, I admit.
Put your nostrils much nearer.
Now, this is a bit tickly:
I don't know quite exactly
What the real diseases are.

1458. Now, what will you give to me
To be cured right properly?
What shall I have, Constantine?
Through the help of my God Sol,
My drink will soon make thee whole,
If I can buy the stuff in time.

Constantine
1464. Look, here are ten pounds for thee
For a start. Now, just heal me
And you shall have even more
All your life: yes, you shall be
A prelate, and never poor.

Doctor
1469. Splendid! These will do some good.
Now, I'll beg leave, if I could,
To go straight home.
I shall come again, Thursday,
With your potions, and I say,
They will heal you. 'Til I come!

he goes down with the clergyman

The Apollonian Bishop waits in the same place

1475. I didn't lift a finger,
Yet I've not had a better
Payment, by my dear God Sol.
But, my God, if I only
Knew how to cure it wholly!
I need to live, above all.
Now, falsehood helps us solely,
When physicians rise, and fall.

Cleric
1483. I don't know a better herb
Than falsehood is, by my word,
For successful physicians.

he goes off home

Constantine
1486. Now, Bishop, what do you say?
Except through books, there's no way
To find curing medicines.

Apollonian Bishop
1489. There is not, lord, by my word.
I've been studying a third
Of the year, in the best books.
Now, you will never be whole,
My lord, unless and until
You're washed in blood — that's how it looks.

Prelate
1495. Yes. We have been studying,
And, if you want your healing,
You must be washed in pure blood.
You must not do otherwise,
And that seems to be the size
Of it. It seems not too good.

Constantine
1501. What sort of blood would that be?
No beast in this world spare ye
If the right sort can be found.
I should be so full of glee
If I could be whole and sound.

Apollonian Bishop
1506. It should not be animal
For him, no. It is needful
To use the blood of children,
Gathered from all the country,
The suckling ones especially.
Pure blood they should all have, then,
Which excels ointments, you see,
And you shall be whole again.

Prelate

1514. Send soldiers to the country,
To gather several sundry
Children up — say, three thousand.
And let their pure blood be saved
In that clean vessel you have,
When they have been slain. How grand
When you are washed therein. Brave,
White as crystal, understand.

Constantine

1522. Well, I think we may do it.
Come here, Torturers, to it
At once! Come quickly to me!
Come on, torturers, to it!
Wake up! Wake up! Come to me.

First Torturer   *to Constantine*

1527. Hail, my dear Lord Constantine.
Rascal and noble consign
Themselves to thee. We are come.
If you wanted something good,
You would not have called us, would
You? What you want now is blood.

The women ready with their children

Constantine

1533. Go for me to the country,
Likewise Rome and the Lombard.
Gather up all the pretty
Little children. Disregard
Any over three years. Hard
It won't be. To this city
Bring them with their mothers. You see,
If there are more, don't discard them.

1541. Let every man go his way.
A portion of armed men, say,

Shall be sent along with you.
He that gathers up the most
Shall get the reward, I boast,
If he gets a hundred or two.

Armed men ready

Second Torturer

1547.   Lord, thy will, it shall be done.
A fourth of the household, come
Along with me right away.
Woman, with thy little child,
And thy neighbour, meek and mild,
To Constantine — not so wild —
Come, or I'll slay thee , I say.

Third Torturer

1554.   Now I have six score children.
Back to the Emperor. Sharpen
Up your knife. These shall be bled
Like a nice porker or calf.
Now, my soldiers, do take half
A care that no woman's fled.

Camp Menial

1560.   I have gathered together
Six score children. Now whether
Enough or not, I've had it!
Troubled are their poor mothers.
When they're dead, there'll be others.
We'll make more sweeties, damn it!

to Constantine with the women and
very many children

1566.   Hail, Constantine in thy tower!
Much travelled for thy pleasure
Am I, about the country.
There are nineteen hundred children.
There will certainly be broken
Hearts when they are slaughtered, see.

Second Torturer
1572. Constantine, I have come
Back here to thee, to thy home,
And have brought six hundred kids.
I am quite ready to bleed
Them, my good lord, yes indeed.
See the dear sweet little babes!

Third Torturer
1578. Hail, Constantine the noble!
The curses of the people
For pleasing thee have I had.
Woe to the child who runs away.
Hearts are broken, so they say.
Eight hundred have I found — aye —
Have them bled at once — be glad.

Camp Menial
1585. Hail, Constantine, in thy tower.
Eleven hundred to thine honour
And more have I now gathered.
Since I went out from my home,
I have made up for thee some
Six or more, let it be said.

First Mother
1591. Oh, pitiless emperor.
If you will here slay these poor
Children who did never sin,
You have received weak counsel.
The God of Heaven evil
Will give to you and your kin.

Justice
1597. Let's not have these big words said.
They shall all soon be dead,
So that we can have their blood.

We must wash thee, Emperor.
He shall be beautified, for
Our learning and our labour
Tell us how to make his skin good.

Constantine

1604.   So now, how many children
Are gathered up for me here?
If I need to slay them, then
I find I must shed a tear.
Their mothers are all wailing,
And I feel pity, I fear.
Health is an important thing
For my body, and most dear.

First Torturer

1612.   Here are three thousand children,
To my knowledge, and seven score.
Let them be killed, don't spare them,

★1615a.   And you shall lose all your sores.
I should kill them in your place,
And I should have no pity —
No more than for a pretty
Hart in the wood, in this case.

Second Torturer

1619.   Oh, I shall bleed a thousand,
And I shall cut all their throats.
We'll make a pile of them and.
Bury them in some remote
Piece of nice ground.
I think no more of killing
A child than of destroying
A goat or a buck, I've found.

Constantine

1627.   There is a duty of kings
In our Rome about such things,
And recorded in our laws.

*This translates a line which W. Stokes omitted in error.

76

Whoever shall kill sucklings
In battle, or kill striplings,
Shall be held cruel. Take pause.
I am not happy to bring
Death to children for my cause.
I know not, after dying,
Into what pain the soul withdraws.

Third Torturer
1637. Emperor, let them be slain
Now, so that you may be healed.
If God won't help, I maintain,
The Devil's good in this field.
Now after this,
Wash yourself in all their blood,
If you want to be healed good.
Let us slay them here — oh bliss.

A Menial
1645. What loss is it for slaying
This little girl and boy — chits —
In one night, so I'm saying,
I could make nine of these twits,
Sort of thing.
If you wish, O sovereign lord,
I'll cut their throats with the sword,
And bleed them, without thinking.

The Torturers go off and the women wait in the open

Constantine
1653. Oh sweet darlings of your mums,
The wrong of it overcomes
Me — to be slain for my sake.
It's a pity, you know,
To slay three thousand children so,
Just for me. It's a mistake.

1659.   Oh, I would much sooner die
        With a terrible disease.
        I just cannot justify
        Killing three thousand to ease
        The suffering that is my
        Lot. Cruelty would displease
        Everybody and would buy
        More suffering, to slay these.

1667.   Give the children to their mums.
        On pain of hanging and drawing,
        I charge that no-one here comes
        To killing or to slaying
        A child. I shall
        Give money to the women
        To buy food and drink, and then
        I will give to the children
        Good raiment. Now, citizen,
        Nurse your children as you will.

Second Mother
1677.   Emperor, great thanks to you
        For showing so much pity
        Towards us poor dear women.
        The children are saved. May God
        Vouchsafe health to you, my Lord.
        Thankyou for all our children.

Constantine
1683.   Now I will go to my bed.
        Darkness has soon overspread
        The sky. Oh, I am weary

        Of my life. If I had health,
        I'd give my kingdom itself,
        And all my chattels, freely.

let him close the door

Jesus

1689. Peter and Paul, by divine
Decree, go to Constantine
Upon the earth. Through pity
Which he had for the children,
Silvester, it is certain,
Shall make him once more healthy.

Peter

1695. Lord, we shall do as you will.
Brother Paul, let us fulfil
Our duty to Constantine.
For he spilt not
Of blood one spot,
He shall be healed, I divine.

Peter and Paul descend
Constantine goes up to the tower

Paul

1701. Constantine, are you sleeping?
Listen to us both: healing
Is what we are sent for now.
Because pity soon did spring
Into your heart for darling
Children, Christ will soothe thy brow.

Peter

1707. Yes, because thou didst not spill
Blood of innocents, Christ will
Begin to heal thee through us.
We'll soon have thee on the mend.
Quickly to Silvester send.
He'll come and cure thee — no fuss.

Constantine

1725. Benedicte, what a sight
I had in the night. There came
To me two men — very bright —

The door shut fast: all the same,
Entered and said
To send after Silvester.
I should be healed — no bother.
And all while I was abed.

1733.   Messenger, please, with great haste,
Send Silvester to me. Waste
No time. Tell him to come here.
He is on Mount Soracte,
Hiding with all his clergy.
Tell him to come without fear.

Second Messenger   *(to Constantine)*
1739.   My Lord Constantine, thy will
Shall always be fulfilled
By me in quite a short space.
Now, my dear knights, come to me.
I do not quite know where he
On the mountain may be traced.

(to Silvester on Mount Soracte)

Hail Silvester and clergy.
Hide no more — you shall be free.
Stay no more in this same place.

The images of Peter and Paul ready with Silvester

1748.   To Constantine, emperor,
You must go, right away, for
He has ordered it, you see.

Silvester
1751.   May Heaven's Lord be worshipped,
For now I am well assured,
We shall all in fellowship
Suffer death for our dear Lord.
We can't refuse.

to Constantine

1759.   Hail Constantine, in thy tower.
        I know that thou deservest
        That honour in this hour.
        Oh, thy belief is manifest,
        I do suggest.
        You are an unbeliever,
        And for that, you'll die in fear.
        I can't bow to thee, I confess.

he goes up

Constantine
1767.   Silvester, you are welcome.
        You have not done a bad deed.
        To me you were asked to come.
        Don't fear reproof — there's no need.
        I am diseased, and the sum
        Of it is, my clergy feed
        On it. Day and night there's one
        Or other of all that breed
        Who counsel me,
        Three thousand children to slay,
        That I should then bathe and stay
        In that same warm blood all day.

1779.   Three thousand were gathered here
        To do the job — this I fear.
        I had pity — could not besmear
        Myself with this blood — oh dear —
        Not just for me.
        I ordered them to go home,
        But at night, there came
        To me a vision, you see.

1787.   Two men came to me at night,
        When all the doors were shut close.
        They were filled with such great might,
        Well — who they were, no-one knows,
        My goodness, no!

They told me that I was to
Send for Silvester, and so
I should be without woe.
"He shall wash thee clean before
He goes, and you shall be healed."
Who can these people be? Sore
Am I to have this revealed.
Tell me, Silvester.
They were two gods, so they were.

Silvester

1801. No, it is not possible
That they were gods, Constantine.
They were two dear apostles
Of Christ, the true Lord divine.
Here I have their several
Images in portraits fine.
I'll give you their names in full.
To do that I shan't decline.

Constantine

1809. By the soul of my body!
They were the same exactly.
Look, that one there with the keys,
And his friend there, with the sword.
They were with me, by my word.
I have never seen nor heard
Better in all my days. Please —
Mercy upon Christ! Record
This: I'll be a Christian lord.

Silvester

1818. I'll make thee a catechumen.
So — thou'lt do penance, then,
For one whole week, without fail.
After that, thou'lt be baptized
And washed clean; and here's the prize:
Thou shalt be healed and made whole.

Constantine

1824. This is truly my desire,
To call upon Christ, for there
Is mercy for all my sin.
Atonement I shall now seek,
And to orphans and the weak,
Alms-giving I shall begin.

Silvester   *he descends. Holy Water ready*

1830. And now I shall baptize thee
In the name of sweet Mary,
And in the name of her Son.
Now thou art washed clean, may He
Who died upon the cross-tree,
Grant you healing, everyone.

the mask away

*When he went down into the water of baptism, there shone
forth a marvellous splendour of light. So thence he came
forth clean, and declared that he had seen Christ.*

Jesus

1836. Constantine, for thy pity
Which you had for the children,
And for thine own dear mercy,
When you just would not slay them

(the procession ready)

I will surely heal thee
When thou art truly washen.
Whoever shall have mercy,
My mercy shall heal him then.

Constantine

1844. Benedicte! What a light
There was here some time ago.
Jesus Christ in all his might

Have I seen, and that is so.
His wounds were all open, right
In front of my eyes, I know.
I saw them all. What a sight.
And he did comfort me too.

Silvester

1852. Well may you be so happy.
You were a leper really,
But thanks to Christ, you are healed.
There's no fairer
Man, nor sweeter,
To my knowledge, that's revealed.

Constantine

1858. I give thanks to Christ Jesu,
Also to thee, Silvester.
To thy palace, it is I who
Will be the chief processor.
And I will command that no
God be worshipped, not ever,
But Christ; and if I live, true
Belief in Jesus' laws forever.

To the Pope's palace in procession, and thereafter
let him go home

SECOND PART — MERIASEK PLAY

Outlaws shall parade here, or one representing all

First Outlaw

1866. I am an outlaw in the
Forest. Never have I had a
Better time in all my days.
When my stuff at home's diminished,
I get some more, 'til that's finished.
Robbery's all sport and play.

Second Outlaw

1872. It's now time to look for prey.
Our money's all gone, by my fay.
So, come on then, dear Master.
Look out for a chap, if you can,
With a heavy purse: a churchman.
They'll soon collect more, after.

First Outlaw

1878. Up, comrades! Let's be off. Watch out,
With all your might, for a good stout
Wandering merchant. Don't refrain
From laying hold of him. And then
Don't fret, I'll take care of you men,
And uphold you, time and again.

Third Outlaw

1884. I see a bloke on horseback.
I'll have a go or I'll crack.
Now look at this, I've got him!
Get down, pal. I'll have, of course,
Your heart's own purse, and your horse.
I'll have them sharpish — on a whim.

Merchant

1890. Listen to me, gentlemen.
Dread the evil to your soul when
You pass away from this earth.
Your spirit will surely pay
In pain and misery, I say.
Then woe betide the soul's dearth.

the priest ready

First Outlaw

1896. When hast thou seen a human soul
Left on the hedge repenting so
For its sin? The way I thought,
For sure, if God won't take me,
The Devil will, and gladly:
As merrily as a hawk.

Fourth Outlaw

1902. There's a chap in a long gown.
I think that's a priest there, down
The road. That one's got loot.
Bona dies, parson sir,
We'll swop purses, as it were,
By my faith, before we scoot.

Priest

1908. Oh, thou man, think of thy God.
His way is not to be trod
By doing this. Infallibly,
You break his commandments, and
You know enough to understand
This, and not be so silly.

First Outlaw

1914. He who has fear of his God
Will never prosper, poor sod,
Wherever he goes. Don't set

Yourself up against us, mate,
But hand over all your plate,
Or I'll quarter thee, don't fret.

Priest
1920. All I have is given to you.
The time is coming when the true
Facts between us will be sorted
Out by Jesus Christ, and you few
Will pay, the truth reported.

First Outlaw
1925. Shall we be getting credit
Until Doomsday? As we shan't be
In the flesh — and you said it —
Thou shalt lose more from thy body.
Strip off his cloth!
We've got long enough to pay.
When Judgement is, he can't say.
Until then, we shan't pay it off.

Second Outlaw
1933. There he is, in naked fashion.
This should always be the ration
For blokes who've got more than enough.

they wait in the Place

Count Rohan
1936. I am Rohan, Paramount
Lord, a very honoured earl.
Now, my troubles all amount
To Meriasek, a churl
Who went away,
Forsook his parents, my relations,
Went without explanations:
I'm very angry, I must say.

First Messenger

1944. Sir Count, mighty Lord, indeed,
Meriasek has come — take heed —
Back again, to our country.
He can actually be seen
Near a place called Pontelyne.
He's a hermit there, you see.

Count Rohan

1950. My intent is now to go
To him, with me his friends also.
We'll see if we can persuade
Him to return to his share
In this world. His kinsmen care,
And are angry, I'm afraid.

Kinsman of Count Rohan

1956. He is on a great mountain,
A thousand paces from the bottom —
Or that is what I have heard.
And there, at all times, night and day,
Goes his solitary way,
With little food — take my word.

The Count goes down towards the Mountain;
also a relative of the Father, and a relative
of the Mother

Meriasek

1962. Thanks be to Jesus. Here am I
Dwelling in the wilderness by,
Thus living like a hermit.
In place of my clothes of silk,
Fine purple cloths and such ilk,
I now wear a grey garment.

1968. A horsehair shirt next is mine.
I drink not cider nor wine,
Mere water for beverage.

The plants from the brooks I eat,
They're sufficient for my meat,
Lest the self remain savage.

Agnate (Kinsman on Meriasek's Father's side)
1974. Meriasek is over here,
Worshipping almighty God, clear
On the top of the mountain.
It is thought by old people
That from here to the chapel
Is a thousand paces, certain.

Count Rohan
1980. Meriasek, joy to thee!
Come to visit thee are we,
And to give thee some solace.
Also, we would make it known
That thy nearest kin make moan
Because thou art in this place.

Meriasek
1986. Why should they be making moan?
To my knowledge, I have done
No harm to any of them,
Nor to any man on earth,
Nor, for all that I am worth,
Would I, with the help of Heaven.

Count Rohan
1992. A great pity 'tis for thee,
Raised of such great family,
That thou shouldst so simply wish
To be here in such trouble.
Thus, thou art friendless: doubly
So, I dare to say — so, pish!

Meriasek
1998. For me, it's good
To draw near God
And worship Him;

To do his will,
Yes, to the fill,
And inherit Heaven's kingdom.

Cognate (or Kinsman) of Count Rohan

2004.   Thou couldst worship God, I say,
As do many men today,
Handsomely and decently
Living. So come now with us.
I am sorry — oh alas! —
That thy life here is beastly.

Meriasek

2010.   Poverty on God's behalf
Is advancement in the Hereafter's
Court, and this
Also a mother of healing.
You do not know, my children,
What the food of the soul is.

Count Rohan

2016.   Meriasek, you're not wise.
Thou canst worship God *and* despise
All the world's greatest honour.
Thine own dear ones suffer shame,
You put yourself here, with *your* name,
Saying nothing, like a beggar.

Meriasek

2022.   Beware your trespass, O people.
Mine will be life so noble
In time to come.
For the soul, sheer nourishment
'Tis, to achieve fulfilment
Of salvation.

2028.   It drives out the lust of the flesh,
And the world it banishes,
Treading it under its feet.
It never does harm to man.

The Devil's power always can
Be confounded by this neat
Trick. Thus, nourishment for man's
Soul, and the joy of Heaven complete.

Count Rohan
2036. There are surely many men
Who would like to go to Heaven,
And yet they have worldly wealth.
In the same way, thou couldst do
Honour to thy family too,
And save thyself.

Meriasek
2042. I shall never love worldly
Wealth, riches or dignity.
No, by my faith I shall not!
Deceptive and untrustworthy
Are they. Though thou hast plenty,
Beware of what thou hast got.

Agnate
2048. Do not tempt his man again.
Christ, the Dear Heart, requires of men
Faithful service.
If he were not a true saint,
Clearly, he could not acquaint
Us with miracles.   *(pronounce* **miraclys***)*

Count Rohan
2054. I will not worry him, no.
It does not concern me — though —
Meriasek, I pray thee,
Do one thing for me, for so
Thou art my blood.
There are robbers in this country,
Putting an end to many
A man. Make them go away,
Since thy power is great and good.

2063.   No man can go to a fair
         Without his being robbed there —
         Ruined in body and wealth.
         I should surely like to see
         Fairs in all of Brittany,
         If thou wilt give me some help.

2069.   Now, the sixth day
         That's in July,
         Call the first fair.
         The next, I'll say,
         August, say I —
         On the eighth, dare
         I have my way.
         And the third in September —
         Thus, Michael's feast remember.
         These same fairs shall forever
         Be held in Noyal, for aye.

Meriasek
2080.   This shall to thee be granted,
         As is by thee desired,
         Through the grace of God alone.
         The robbers shall be banished —
         Some to their own advantage,
         If through God's mercy they atone.

First Outlaw
2086.   Now, my dear mates, look about.
         If you happen to see out
         There, some fellow wandering
         By the woods: quick! Guide his purse
         To me. He shall get God's curse,
         Who'er speaks against robbing!

                    Hereupon, a fire comes upon them

Second Outlaw
2092.   Oh! Woe to us, great and small.
         The whole wood's on fire. We'll all

Be burnt to ashes. Now's come
To us a great misfortune,
And that's for the importune
Devilry on earth that we've done.

Third Outlaw
2098. Be quiet, Devil burn thee!
Why — what is all the hurry,
And the dreadful capering?
You see a brightness — I know
It is merely from the glow
Of the dear moon there — rising.

Fourth Outlaw
2104. Help! Help! Run! Run!
The wood is gone   *(a horse ready)*
Up in a proper great blaze!
Help! I'll get out if I can.
We'll all be burnt up, to a man.
We're all going to be scalded.
Ah! God curse this job! Which way's
My horse? I hope the Devil pays
This jet black steed, and it falls dead!

Let the fourth outlaw pass by (and go off) on the horse

First Outlaw
2113. Oh! Meriasek, Meriasek,
As thou art a mighty saint,
Pray now for me.
Let me not be burnt in fire,
And I shall be, my entire
Life long, a servant to thee.

Second Outlaw
2119. Meriasek, please save me,
I ask, without flattery.
If what I have heard is true,

That thou art mighty,
Then thou might'st well see,
I will ever follow you.

he ends

Third Outlaw
2125. Meriasek, a true saint,
Save my life! Oh, I shall faint.
I offer my life to you.

Fifth Outlaw
2128. In Meriasek I believe,
And for my foetid sins I grieve.
I shall be a servant true.
As he is mighty, achieve
This I shall. Mercy, Jesu.

First Outlaw
2133. Thanks to Meriasek, see:
Well and truly saved are we
From harm; and thanks to Jesus.
We'll go to him right away,
And we will ask him to say
Prayers to Christ, to forgive us.

to Meriasek on the Mountain

2139. Meriasek, joy to thee!
Here we are, now come to see
If thou wilt give us advice.
We have been men without grace.
Our business has been to chase
And rob people: a great vice.

2145. One day, we were in the wood,
Intent on plundering good,
Respectable people. Then,

A blast of fire came on us:
Real lightening! We thought it was
Truly for us all, our end.

2152. I cried out piteously,
"Oh, Meriasek, help me!"
I was saved by that alone.
Saved were some of all my band.
Others fled on either hand.
Some, I know not where they've gone.
Here am I, put out, unmanned:
Damned, perhaps, and all alone.

Meriasek
2160. For mercy of Jesus pray,
And remember God alway.
Take care that you be shriven.
To Jesus Christ will I pray
For you, very readily.
Do not to sin be driven.

First Outlaw
2166. Meriasek, Meriasek,
Take pity on the poor, sick
Souls, if it is possible.
If we had not cried on thee,
We'd have been lost, young and grey.
Oh, it has been terrible.

Meriasek
2172. Never fall into despair.
Dear God is merciful where
People pray to him. I see
You are repentant and true,
Therefore, I will bless you.
In nomine patris et filii
Et spiritus sancti amen.
Let your restitutions be
To as many as you can, then.

Count Rohan

2180. Now, be great thanks to Jesus,
And to Meriasek too.
All is made quiet for us,
For all the rich and poor who
Will want to go to the fairs.
The robbers are all surely
Gone far off from the country.
This is the end of our cares.

2188. Thanks to our mighty Jesus!
Through Meriasek's prayer was
All this. The three fairs shall be
Held. Meriasek granted
Them. Now let him be worshipped.
A fair shall certainly be
Held, the sixth of July,
According to my wish. My
Second fair, definitely
Shall be held on the eighth day
Of August, and shall always
Be held in the country.
Now the third, perpetually
On Michaelmas Day, we shall see
In September. Then, blessed
Meriasek's name shall be
In Noyal, let it be said.

Duke of Cornwall *parades, saying:*

2205. Of all Cornwall, Duke am I,
As was also my father.
A great lord in the country,
From Land's End to the Tamar.
I am dwelling in — no lie —
Castle an Dinas itself,
In Pydar.
And up on the high ground,

The Duke of Cornwall

A Tyrant

I've another castle sound,
Which is named Tintagel,
Where my chief dwelling is found.

2216.　I am told that in the Hundred
Of Penwith there is a most
Saintly man — so it is said.
He arrived here from the coast,
Not far away.
Steward — have you really read
Of him, I pray?

The Duke's Steward

2224.　Indeed I have, mighty Lord.
Meriasek is he called.
A saintly man in his ways,
He is loved by everyone.
Also, much good here he's done
In the country — so they say.

The Duke's Chamberlain

2230.　Lord, I will tell you truly,
He's gone to another country,
It must be a week ago.
He has quite definitely
Not been seen by anybody
Within Cornwall — that is so.

Duke

2236.　Why has he left the country?
In all his days a very
Good man he was. I never
Heard tell anything different.
Many with great argument
Praise him for his goodness ever.

2242.　Teudar, that impious man,
Landed in this country, pagan
That he is; and as you know,
That was only recently.

He can't bear Christians, certainly
Anywhere near him; and so,
Meriasek's forcibly
Been driven out: made to go.

The Duke of Cornwall
2250. Fie on the dirty dog. Fie!
Why was I not informed of it?
By God who put me in this world, I'll
Shorten his wind a little bit.
Before Wednesday night he will try
Sorrow's acquaintance. He'll be fit
To chatter his teeth awhile
Over his inflamation, I wyt.

2258. My retinue, be at hand!
I'll not have within my land
A dog like this. He shall pay
For it, and quite severely.
If he will not turn and flee,
His blood shall run to ground, I say.

The Duke's Steward
2264. We are all prepared, your grace.
A lot of harm's taken place
Since he came to this country.
In Meneage, at Lesteudar,
That's where his headquarters are,
Rallying to him are many.

Duke of Cornwall
2270. Even a hundred thousand
Of them will go to their death and
That by the will of Jesus
Above. I want to know why
He came to this country, my
Leave not applied for. Let us
All go together and try
To find out in good heart — we must.

The Duke descends with twenty armed men with streamers

2278. Tell me, my lords, which is the best
Course to keep, to meet with the pest,
The Tyrant? If I'm able,
For his undoubted badness,
He shall be rendered powerless
Through the faith of Christ. He'll fare ill.

Steward
2284. He was living in Lesteudar,
That is a place in Meneage.
The ill-born man has another
Dwelling for all his intrigue:
That's in Powder.
Now, that place is called Goodern.
It is near there, the rotten
Man has made himself a harbour.

Duke
2292. So, we will keep to the south,
In the name of Christ above.
If he lives in Cornwall, no doubt
We'll meet the villain soon enough.
And now my banner break out
Before me, as it behoves
A noble lord to go about
The business with Christian love.

Second Messenger   *(to Teudar)*
2300. Hail Teudar, noble emperor!
There is, in the kingdom here,
A duke, risen against thee.
And with him there's a great host
Of people, willing to boast
That your death he'll surely see.

Emperor Teudar

2306. Out with him, the false dirty
Villain. Day and night I defy
Him. Against him I'm too strong.
Their beards will start to tremble.
Executioners, assemble!
To arms! Forward! Woe to wrong!

First Executioner

2312. Ready are we, all in arms.
Their beards shall shake in alarm,
Those who dare set against thee.
If there is need to engage
With the Devil himself, I'll wage,
He won't joust with us — not he.

Teudar

2318. To the field, by the Devil!
Let us go, and no blessing
Of ourselves. They'll pay! I'll level
The Duke and his following
Before I leave work. By my soul,
Rum ena, there is a whole
Fifteen thousand on my roll
Of people. We'll take some toll!

Descends with fifteen armed men, with streamers

First Demon

2326. Peace, I say, both far and near.
Listen now to Jupiter,
Holy Father of the North.
My servants are coming here.
We'll put them right, never fear,
On the road and send them forth!

Second Demon, Beelzebub

2332. Well done, Master. Teudar will
Do enough of his evil,

If we want to encourage
Him. Let's go to the temple.
Well, to me it's quite simple:
Let all wickedness flourish.

let him go into the temple

Teudar
2338. Joy to thee, O God Moufras,
I wish to beseech thy grace
On the battlefield.
Now, I don't wish
To do good. This
I wouldn't dream of — no, indeed.

First Demon
2344. Go forth like a man, Teudar,
And spare your evil never.
I'll sustain thee.
Thy soul shall not go to waste,
I've a pit for it, just in case;
Likewise for your soldiers. Face
It, be happy!

The more good lives you've ended,
The more you'll be commended,
And praised hereafter — you'll see.

First Torturer
2354. Come on! Let's be off at once.
Doesn't matter what we chance,
Mahound owns us — we're not free.

Steward
2357. My Lord, there's Teudar, I tell
You, with a wicked parcel
Of people following him.
Do you wish to speak and ask
What is his real and proper task
In this country — or leave him?

Duke of Cornwall

2363. Indeed I wish to ask it.
Although there be black magic
In him, I will never fear.
Though they are pretending strength,
I shall feel their faces' length.
And be roaring at their rear.

to the stalls

2369. Thou tyrant disbeliever!
What is thy right in this country?
Thou hast not title nor claim here,
I can see that, obviously,
On father or mother's side.
Thou hast put out of the kingdom,
Meriasek, acclaimed by one
And all a good man — I'll tan thine hide!

Teudar

2377. Before I go, I'll put thee out
Of the country, like the despised
Meriasek if, like that lout,
Thou worshippest that mouth of lies,
Who bore cruel pains
On a certain old cross-tree,
Called Jesus. And now, certainly,
Taking vengeance and other gains
From his servants here you see me.
Come on, mouth of frost, feel your pains.

The Duke

2387. That does not lie in thy power,
False, excommunicated dog.
I shall spill thy blood sooner,
And thou shalt be chopped up, thou hog,
Like little greens,
To make broth, by my dear soul.
Rum ena! Thou wast, I am told,

103

An ostler's boy, a groom, it seems.
Is the Devil's son so bold
To take vengeance on Cornwall's schemes?

Teudar
2397. I will crush the Duke of Cornwall
Under my feet, with all his people,
Just like little grains of sand.
While my property was not
Large in my nation, I've got
Quite a bit now in my hand.
A proven conqueror am I,
A person of substance: that's why
I'm feared amongst lords in this land.

Duke
2406. I do not care about thy might,
Thou tyrant, not a one-eyed bean.
If you don't get off my land right
Away, I'll run thee through clean
To the heart. Undoubtedly,
I think thou wast an evil wretch
In thy country. Now you fetch
Yourself from my sight, dog. Catch
It from me or ask mercy.

2415. What fine alien
Upon Christians
Presumes to set himself here?
I will make thine head a pulp,
So that the juice will soon gulp
Out. You: "Sadly met" and "Oh dear."

Teudar
2421. Oh dear me! The poor gadfly
Would kill a horse if it could.
Just like you, gudgeon, you'd try
To do harm to me, if I would
Only let you.

I certainly shan't stand quiet,
Good-for-nothing. Don't deny it —
Royal sovereignty will hie it
Here to my aid, and that's true.

Duke
2430. Thy accursed sovereignty
Shall be of precious little help.
Call the great, the humble — let's see
Thy common horsemen gallop,
And all thy "lords."
On the field I shall await you,
As I am a servant faithful
To Christ, and to all my wards.

Teudar
2438. Thou vile blockhead!
Not a word said
About that Christ
In front of me,
Or we shall see
If shame suffice
Your army — for
What? Do you hope
To really cope
In battle with an Emperor?

Duke
2448. Yah! Thou false mischief-maker.
That thou wast a landowner
In this world I didn't know.
Don't presume, dirty alien,
Upon my inheritance, then,
Day or night. You shan't hold sway so.

2454. For meddling with good men,
Such as Meriasek, then,
Thou shalt come off much the worse.
Yes: *re an jeth brus uthek*

I'll give it thee in the neck,
Stable-lad. You're bad, and cursed.

Teudar
2460. Lord Duke, thy faith thou shalt deny,
Or else a prisoner of my
Own thou shalt be, before night.
King Alwar and Pygys too,
Noble King Mark — he also,
And King Casvelyn, you know,
Are coming with troops: that's right.

Duke
2467. Let them come when they wish to:
They'll amount to little here.
They won't escape without death — no.
By God, great Lord of Grace, though there
Were hundreds of thousands, so
We would withstand you. For, where
There are enemies of Christ, lo,
We'll a battle in his name share.

Teudar
2475. You and Christ I do defy
And all your faith here, as I
Think that you are all rubbish.
They've set themselves against me.
Go and break the Christians' heads. See
What my soldiers can finish.

Duke
2481. Come on then, quick as you like!
In the name of merciful Christ,
I am ready to reply.
At them, my soldiers! They shall
Have quite a story to tell:
Remember us, before they die.

Guns. Here they shall fight

a horse ready

Teudar

2487. My soldiers, bring me a horse.
I cannot withstand their force.
Some of my people are dead,
And badly wounded am I.
The Duke on whom I cried "Fie!"
Is a man unequalled.

Duke

2493. Hold now, my soldiers, now hold!
Taken to flight's the tyrant bold,
Not able to withstand me.
Some of his people are dead:
Glory to the beloved
Christ for granting the victory.

2499. Peace to all, all who are here.
The Life of Meriasek dear
Is revealed in part today.
Come on the second day betimes,
And through the grace of God you'll find,
You'll have the rest of the play.

2505. Come and drink up, everybody,
For the benefit of the play,
I beseech you.
Man and woman, there shall be
The blessing of Christ and Mary
Of Camborne: Meriasek too.
Pipe up, minstrels, heartily,
Let us now some dancing do.

End of First Day's Play.

SECOND DAY OF THE PLAY

DIAGRAM OF ROUND THEATRE

Torturers   Heaven

Hell
          Silvester

Woman's Son
Bishop of   Second Bishop
Apollo
First Magician Duke   Bishop of Cornouailles

Second
Magician   Earl of Vannes
Duke

Earl Globus   King Massen

Tyrant Emperor   Emperor Constantine

Interlude   Silvester Play

On the second day, Emperor Constantine shall parade here saying:

2513.   I am called Constantine,
In Rome, the world's chief city.
The Emperor's crown is mine,
Changed to Christianity
And its doctrine
By Silvester, as you've seen.
I've ordered that there has been
No more worship of unclean
Gods, but that of Christ divine.
He saved us on the cross-tree.

Third Part   Meriasek Play

Here the blind Earl Globus begins, saying:

Earl Globus

2522. Oh God, what now is my worth?
I can see nothing on earth.
My riches are nought but dearth.
To Meriasek lead me,
For I lately heard that he
Does mighty miracles, worth
A fortune to me. I'll see
He's rewarded properly.

Squire

2530. Unto him I will lead you.
We shall speed well, through Jesu.
We'll soon have this business done.
And do, Lord, tell him freely,
How you can't see properly.
Now, let's go up the mountain.

To Meriasek's mountain, led by the Squire
A staff in Earl Globus' hand

The Earl

2536. May the Lord of Heaven help me,
And make me good and healthy.

Meriasek

2538. May the Lord who made the land
And the sea, always help me,
And guide me by his own hand,
To make my life here happy.
Lord Jesu, grant me thy grand,

Unfailing Grace. Look on me.
Jesu, I have always planned
In this world to please just thee.

The Earl
2546. Meriasek, joy to thee.
A good man of thy converse
Thou art accounted, truly
All over the universe
Art named a gracious priest. We
Know you help the needy, cursed,
Rich and poor, bad and greedy,
Sick and dying and much worse.

2554. A blind man who does not see,
Before I presume to speak,
I tell you I'll repay thee,
If it stands in my power. Weak
Of sight I be,
Unable to help myself.
If you can stop my ill-health,
You shall never lack the wealth
Of this world. I'll give freely.

Meriasek
2563. The wealth of the world concerns
Me not. A man quickly learns
That wealth is just a phantom.
It gives very poor returns.
Wealth offers you no ransom.

The Earl
2568. It seems to me a wonder
That the riches of the world
You hate. Neither you nor other
Men could live long, nor any churl,
Without wealth. Through riches made
Conversant with prince, duke or earl,
By all the people obeyed —
Treated like a precious pearl.

2576. Ask all that you want of me,
Meriasek, you shall see.
From now on, you'll lack nothing.
A hundred pounds would be cheap
If I could get just one peep
Out of my eyes — anything.

Meriasek
2582. It is not for man to buy,
My dear son, this Grace of God.
Unto the world from on high
It comes. *What way* have you trod?

The Earl
2586. To give wealth bothers me not.
If I could only just see,
I'd argue with a king. What
Else wouldn't I do to be
Fit and able? It's better
To have all my sight back than
Have ten pounds worth of land.
Take the title and letter.

Meriasek
2594. All thy promise and thy lands,
Keep them now as before.
I shall do as Christ commands,
The head of the saints, for sure.

The Earl
2598. I beseech, wholeheartedly,
For love of the great Passion
Which Jesus bore, please save me.
Scourged in most dreadful fashion
By the Jews, nailed, feet and hands,
A sharp spear was his ration:
See where the hardest blow lands!
This was the Lord's great Passion.

2606. Right through the heart.
How it did smart,
And the blood flew.
Heal a blind man,
Soon as you can,
For love of Jesu.

Meriasek

2612. For the love of sweet Jesu,
If only you prayed before,
Cured of it you would be too.
I hold your riches no more
Valuable than a bean.   *he kneels*
Jesus Christ, merciful might,
Jesus Christ, restore the sight
Of this man. Let us be seen.

The Earl   *(kneels)*

2620. May Jesu, our mighty Lord,
Be worshipped now, forever.
Also Meriasek, glorious
Saint, who saved me altogether.
Now I see, beautifully.
I have never seen clearer.
As we know, lettered and lay,
No servant of God is dearer.

The Demoniac

2628. Oh Meriasek, help me,
For love of the dear Jesu.
I am vexed, as you see,
By an evil spirit. True —
My life is through.
With such scourings it takes me,
I'd rather be burnt completely
Than have to endure it so.

A Deaf Man

2636. I am one who cannot hear.
Meriasek, worthy, dear,

I am thinking you could cure
Me. I very much do fear.
For love of Christ we revere,
Look upon us fellows poor.

he kneels

Meriasek
2642. Jesus Christ, through thy mercy,
If there's an evil spirit,
Jesu, send him off safely,
And give us healing here. It
Is for these men.
Let them all know,
On earth I go,
Serving thee, then.

The Demon
                                      (the Demonic howls)
2650. Meriasek, out on thee!
Now thou art accursed to me,
Driving me from this country.
Because of you I have no peace,
But I will quickly sow disease
For your sake, liar, then you'll see.

Demoniac
2656. Thanks be to the Lord Jesus.
The evil spirit from us
Is certainly gone. I see.
I am well. I have no strife.
Meriasek, all my life
I am truly bound to thee.

The Deaf Man
2662. Yes, and I can
Hear, just like you.
I am fit, and
I am bound to

Meriasek.
I am healed through
His good prayers too.
Meriasek!

Earl Globus
2670. Meriasek, ever honoured,
By you are we comforted,
Who were so greatly in need.
You have brought us so much joy.
Now we shall forever pray.
May Christ keep thy power indeed.

Meriasek
2676. My sweet children, go you home.
My blessing, wher'er you roam.
Do not keep me from my task.
Give thanks to God, and be sure,
He has given you your cure.
He works through me. I just ask.

all go home

Here the Earl of Vannes parades

The Earl of Vannes
2682. I am the great Earl of Vannes,
A Lord, great in dignity.
The greatest of my commands
Is, worship thy God, humbly.
May you be given
Enough Grace to sustain it.
Now, the Bishop has snuffed it.
Who will get his living?
There is a college here, fit
To replace the one in Heaven.

A Squire of the Earl of Vannes
2692. Sir Lord, we will go with you.
Not much happens here, it's true,

Without your interference.
Both the rich and the poor are
Thinking, Meriasek far
Exceeds all others. It makes sense.

The Earl of Vannes *(to the dean in the college on*
2698. Sir Dean, joy to you, I say, *the scaffold-stage)*
And to your college today.
I've come for your opinion.
Who do you think ought to be
The new Bishop — you tell me.
So: who has now been chosen?

The Dean *(on the stage)*
2704. Sir Earl, worthy Lord, my dear,
You are surely welcome here.
We're glad to have *your* advice.
We want to know — make it clear —
Who shall be Bishop. Don't fear,
We'll announce it in a trice.

The Earl of Vannes
2710. All the common people are
For Meriasek. He far
Exceeds all others in that.
I know of no-one better,
Do you? I don't know whether
You want to have a longer chat?

the Earl goes home

The Canon
2716. We are certainly joyous,
Meriasek is for us,
As our primate.
We are not disappointed.
Send for his bulls. Appointed
Without debate.

The Earl of Vannes

2722. Come forward, my messenger.
Go now to Pope Silvester.
Tell him that the very chiefs
Of Brittany are asking
For Meriasek. We'll bring
Him here at once, for we sing
His praises here. That's in brief.

First Messenger   *(to the Earl of Vannes)*

2729. You won't be disappointed,
Sir Earl, he'll be appointed.
I'll bring his papal bulls home.
I won't delay.
I'm on my way.
Farewell, I'm off now to Rome.

Silvester

2735. The blessing of the Father
Be with us all forever.
Jesu of Grace, in the evening
Succour us, and in the morning.
The holy blessed Spirit
Be with us, and remit
Our sins, through Mary, Mother
And Virgin. Hear now our prayer.

2743. God's mercy is forever sure
For those who seek. The Creator
Has never wanted to lose
What he has redeemed. So choose
To stand and be clean confessed.
Avoid sin in this world. It's best.
And for the sin already done,
Make full repentance, everyone.
And then beware.
Be sure you turn to sin no more.
For then, you shall come to Heaven
To share in joy that has no end.

First Messenger

2755.　Honour to you, Silvester.
　　　My Lord, I have been sent here
　　　From Brittany, dear master.
　　　We should like your permission
　　　Now for the consecration
　　　Of Meriasek. It's clear,
　　　The Lords have the intention
　　　To give him Vannes, I hear.

Silvester

2763.　Thou art welcome, my dear son.
　　　Meriasek's a good man,
　　　Or so I have heard it said.
　　　His bulls shall be made ready,
　　　So that your return journey
　　　Shan't be fruitless. They'll be read.

Bulls ready

A Cardinal　　　　　　　　　　*to the Messenger*

2769.　The Papal bulls are now ready.
　　　Messenger, take them to thee,
　　　By my own good Lord's licence.
　　　They say that he
　　　Is so good, we
　　　Should learn from his own prudence.

First Messenger

2775.　My good Lord, much thanks to you.
　　　The thing that I had to do
　　　Was by your help made easy.
　　　And now, I pray,
　　　Upon my way,
　　　I must go, to my country.

Silvester

2781.　Now, Christ's blessing go with thee.
　　　Greet the Lords of your country,

For Meriasek and us.
Loyally will he serve you,
A shepherd never more true
Nor ever one more pious.

The Messenger   *(to the Earl of Vannes)*
2787. Hail, Sir Earl there, in your tower!
The business which, by your power,
Took me away, is now done.
Please take Meriasek's bulls.
When I spoke of my purpose,
They all praised him, everyone.

The Earl of Vannes
2793. Messenger, you are welcome.
To the wilderness, all and some,
Meriasek us to seek.
And take the letters with you.
The chiefs of the country too,
Nothing but good of him speak.

The Dean
2799. Lord, all of that shall be done.
Let us go then, everyone,
To Meriasek.
Now he's in the wilderness.
He can leave there. It is best
To him seek.

to Meriasek's mountain

2805. Meriasek, oh great joy!
A letter needing reply
For you to read.
See how every living Lord
Wants you for Vannes, in accord:
Wants you for Bishop indeed.

Meriasek

2811. My great thanks to all the Lords,
And you, the canons. Record
This: I don't want the honour.
I don't want charge of a cure
In this world. Of this I'm sure,
Not whilst I'm alive — never.

A Canon

2817. Meriasek, that's not wise.
Thou shalt have a very nice
Life as a bishop. Honoured
Thou shalt be, and have to spend
Three hundred pounds a year, and
More as well. That's not the end
Of it all, upon my word.

Meriasek

2824. You are like so many men
Of today, who are often
People of the Holy Church.
They work for a benefice,
And then, they ask how it is,
How much money they can work
For themselves here.
They remember not the account
They'll have to give, nor the amount,
When they come to Judgment dear.

2834. All who have a curacy,
Try to remember this now.
Christ will reckon certainly,
The souls, and that I do know.
So consider:
If a fault in the shepherd
Is the one which is *Then* heard,
Woe to him, the poor beggar.

2842. The longer the roll shall be,
       The longer, as you all see,
       It shall be in the reading.
       I never want any cure,
       Except of my soul, that's sure.
       God grant me of it ruling.

The Dean

2848. Let us go home, brethren.
       This man will never listen
       To one who wishes him good.

to the Earl of Vannes

2851. Meriasek refuses
       To be our Father, chooses
       To make that understood.

he goes up and waits in the same place

Earl of Vannes

2854. Alas, what shall we do now?
       Such a marvel he is to
       Us that he should reject it.
       We shall have to think how we
       Can change his mind — pleasantly.
       Otherwise I'll have a fit.

Here the Bishop of Cornouailles parades if he wishes

Bishop of Cornouailles

2860. I'm the Bishop of Cornouailles.
       I'm not being funny —
       Honoured prelate,
       That I am. And now I'll go
       To Vannes. You see, I do so
       Need with other Lords to relate.

The Bishop of Cornouailles' Crozier-Bearer

2866. There is so much to do there.
There is need to take care-
Ful advice from the wise, see?
Who is going to be bishop?
Meriasek gives no sop.
They say the next will be he.

he goes down

Here a second Bishop parades

Second Bishop

2872. Crozier-bearer, come hence:
None of this makes much sense.
We need a Bishop of Vannes,
So, Meriasek they chose.
He won't have it, I suppose,
Although, no doubt, he still can.

Second Crozier-Bearer

2878. Oh my dear Lord, by Saint John,
I'd be glad to have the honour
If they wanted it for me.
I should take all the silver
And double it for the childer.
Entice *me* then, if needs be.

Earl Globus

2884. Bishop of Cornouailles, bonjour.
I have come to see you for
We should go to Vannes this day.

Bishop of Cornouailles

2887. By this day, Sir Earl, welcome.
I'm very glad you have come.
Welcome to you all today.

Second Bishop

2890. My Lord Bishop of Cornouailles,
Many thanks to you, much joy.
We are all bound the same way.
To Vannes we go.
Clearly, there's so
Much to be done, so they say.

Earl Globus   *(to the Earl of Vannes)*

2896. My dear Sir Earl, joy to thee.
Honour to the college be,
Both great and small.
From our home, we have come here
For Meriasek, the dear.
Yes, we would exalt him, all.

Earl of Vannes

2902. Beloved Sir Earl, welcome,
And the Bishops too, welcome.
We have all become ill at ease.
Meriasek was chosen.
Right away, he has given
His refusal, if you please.

all go down with the Earl of Vannes

Bishop of Cornouailles

2908. If his papal bulls have come,
Bishop he shall be, and none
Shall say different.
So, why will he not take it?
He can do much benefit
For all his race — he'll relent.

Second Bishop

2914. Let it be put to him again,
And let's try to set in train
This honour for him.

A man in conversation
Above all of his nation:
Thus has it been said of him.

Earl Globus
2920. Without any more ado,
We shall now just simply go
To the place where he rests,
And we shall bring him from there.
A man most blessed and fair
Is he, amongst their chiefs.

The Bishop of Cornouailles
2926. Yes, on that we all agree.
Let us go, then, verily,
Both small and great,
Old folks, chiefs of the country,
You shall all soon hear our plea,
Learned and lay.

let him go to the hermitage on the mountain

Second Bishop
2932. Look, Meriasek is here.
Sir, Earl, mighty Lord, my dear,
You go and speak to him first.
See if he will come to us
Without trouble or a fuss.
Ruffling him will make it worse.

The Earl of Vannes   *to Meriasek*
2938. Meriasek, joy to thee.
Here, in all humility,
For a long time hast thou stood,
Very much like a poor man.
But now, royalty we plan
For thee, because thou art good.

Earl Globus
2944. A man of conversation
Art thou, amongst thy nation,
And raised of most worthy blood.
You do not live properly,
Staying here in poverty.
Come with us now, if you would.

Second Bishop
2950. Thy papal bulls have come home.
We have the power to make some
Bishop of thee in Vannes too!
Look — this is what we have found —
The country wants it, and you're bound
To think of them, not you.

Meriasek
2956. Do not mention the honour,
For love of dear Christ above,
No. Bishop I will never
Be, and I would never love
To obtain the cure
Of any man or brother
In this world. It is enough
To have my own soul's bother.

Bishop of Cornouailles
2964. Do not seek to bandy words
With us, or try to reverse
What is ordered by the Pope.
Whether you say yes or no,
Away with us you shall go.
Of staying here, there's no hope.

Meriasek   *(Meriasek led)*
2970. Blessed Mary, oh help me!
Blessed Mary, oh, from thee
Against my will am I led.

128

Mary, Mother and Virgin,
Thou knowest well and hast seen,
I'd rather be here instead.

Earl of Vannes

2976. Meriasek, you're not wise.
Somebody must lead — that's the size
Of it. What about the souls?
Where there is a soft shepherd,
The foxes come, take my word,
To lessen the sheep, from their holes.

2982. We are as of one mind on
This. In the church of Saint Sampson
Let him be consecrated,
With pomp and ceremony.
This is not disloyalty,
Meriasek, be not angered.

Meriasek   (*in the Dean's church*)

2988. For love of the Great Passion
The Lord Jesu bore for us,
Nailed by the Jews upon
The cross, feet and hands no less,
A lance in the heart anon,
The thorns of the crown impressed
Into his skull and on,
The blood flowing in a mess
Into his brains:
Now, because I love him so,
I will not be Bishop, no.
I beseech thee, let me go.
Do not longer me detain.

Bishop of Cornouailles

3001. Do not speak vain words alone.
Come now, sit down on thy throne.
Put on thy robe around thee.

Thou shalt be dressed in thy place
As becomes a Bishop of Grace.
Thou shalt lack nothing, I'll see.

Here Meriasek wears a gown

Second Bishop
3007.   Hold thy crozier in thy hand.
In Christ's name of Heaven's land,
And Mary, a Virgin pure.

A crozier of silver and a mitre ready

Set the mitre on his head.
And now, we shall all be glad
Of his coming to the cure.

Bishop of Cornouailles
3013.   Now let's give him a blessing.
May Jesu Christ, according
To his wishes guide thee.
Now th'art head of thy nation.
We've had the installation.
A great day is come, I see.

The Earl of Vannes
3019.   Now we are delighted,
Meriasek's consecrated
Bishop for us.
He is prince of his nation,
Upholder of Salvation,
Spiritual leader for the lost.

Meriasek the Bishop
3025.   This dignity given to me
Seems no more than shame to me,
A shame more than an honour.

I'd be satisfied, really,
Not to have it, oh truly.
For joys I have no desire.

A Naked Sick Man
3031. O good people, God save you.
For love of the dear Passion
Which the Virgin's Son bore. Through
The heart a lance was thrust in.
Both feet and hands were nailed to
A cross, between thieves, I ween.
A diadem of thorns also
For a crown, as may be seen,
So that even to his brain
The thorns themselves went in there.
Give me a garment to wear.
I am naked. The wind is keen.

The Earl of Vannes
3043. O good man, go on your way.
It's not good for you to say
All this in front of the lords,
And you naked and broken.
I have not very often
Seen a filthy man so poor.

The Naked Man
3049. Oh for all the terrible wounds
Which Christ bore, by the nones,
For man's only salvation!
My body is powerless.
My veins are stricken — a mess.
I'm no-one's friend or darling.

3055. Often out in hail and ice
I've been, utterly homeless,
The ground frozen in the night,
My wounds full of filth, useless,
Always burning.

No-one will be my hostess
Or give me a bed. Hopeless
Are my stinking limbs, hurting.

Bishop Meriasek

3063. Thou shalt certainly have clothes,
Though I myself go naked.
I pity to hear thy woes,
Thy flesh rotten and putrid.

The Naked Man

3067. Very great is my sorrow.
I'd wish a fair tomorrow,
But I doubt that. I am faint.
Death will not look upon me.
Now even he avoids me,
Because of my awful taint.

Bishop Meriasek

3073. May Jesu give thee healing,
O thou poor worthy being,
Both in body and in limb.
For all thy affection
To Christ, Lord of Salvation,
Heal this poor man, oh heal him.
Take these clothes, no hesitation.
Cover both body and limb.

(a gown or mantle upon the naked man)

Naked Man

3081. May the mighty Lord, Jesu,
Meriasek, repay you.
Every limb is all healed up.
On my body there's no wound.
Even the rotten flesh soon
Became whole and perfect too.

Earl of Vannes

3087. Meriasek, honour too!
I was not aware that you
Were so mighty in this world.
Worthy of the dignity
Thou art. Everybody home and see
That the truth of this is told.

let him go home, and the Earl's people

Bishop Meriasek

3093. God's blessing now upon you be.
Now I have this dignity,
Given to me here by you,
I would rather give it all
To another man, withal.
God in Heaven knows that's true.

then let all go home

First Leper

3099. Lord of Heaven, what shall I do?
I am very ill, and so,
Nobody will look at me.
Meriasek, I've heard tell,
Makes very sick people well,
Whatever their disease be.
I shall go to him and tell
Him, I need him to help me.

Second Leper

(to Meriasek)

3107. Meriasek, I bless thee.
We, from the community
Are segregated lepers.
I do not need to tell you.
For love of Christ, be it true
That you have healing powers.

133

Meriasek's Chaplain
3113. You stand without, on one side!
This is not for lepers. Hide
Yourselves from the Lord's face.
You should be standing away
From here, awaiting all day
Alms from the worthy man's grace.

Bishop Meriasek
3119. O dear chaplain, no no more.
Do not ever reprove poor
People who may come to me.
I am more ready for them
Than for lords of the kingdom,
Will you not now let me see?

3125. Now, lepers, what do you say?
Have you an errand with me?
Now in the name of God, speak.

First Leper
3128. For love of Heaven, I pray,
Help us from our grief today,
Segregated lepers, weak.
You're a good man,
With a good plan,
To help the people who seek.

Bishop Meriasek
3134. Mary, of all Heaven queen,
Pray with me to Christ of Grace.
Mary, from all this grief seen,
Heal these people's hands and face,
Mary, to whom all have been
In times of trouble, I place
My healing trust in thee, Queen
Of Heaven and full of Grace.

First Leper

3142.   Oh now thanks be to Jesu!
My dear friend, you are healed too,
Clear and fair, both skin and face.

he ends

Second Leper

3145.   And so are you! You are healed too!
Fairer I never saw you.
Now thanks be to Jesus' Grace.
Meriasek, you are blessed.
Now, we are truly impressed.

Bishop Meriasek

3150.   My children, you all go home,
And thank not me, but the one
Who is in the Heaven above.
Believe you this, my children,
Jesus is always helping
With his dear love.

let him go off

THE WOMAN'S SON

(Complete Play)

The Woman Sends Her Son to the King's Court

The Woman Pleads With the Madonna

Here King Massen shall parade

King Massen

3156. Now, I am called King Massen,
A great, bold lord in my day.
To the wilderness, often,
I like to go on Thursday,
For my hunting.
Hunter, make my hounds ready,
Also my household friendly,
Laymen and clerks all with me,
Let's prepare to go hunting.

The King's Hunters

3165. Lord, we shall be ready.
Greyhounds and scent-hounds — let's see:
I have quite a wealth of them.
If we bring a stag to bay,
He'll soon be dead, this I say.
Believe this, then.

Here, the son of a certain woman (as is found in the miracles of the Blessed Mary) shall parade, saying:

3171. For a young man, his duty
Is to be amongst the lords.
There, he learns to be manly,
Learns goodness, his just rewards,
To be the better.
I shall go very gladly,
To the king's court, willingly.
Farewell to you, dear Mother.

he goes down

The Woman, ie. His Mother

3179. Son, the blessing of Mary
Now be with you.
I should be much more happy,

But thus it goes,
If you stayed with me,
At home and not with others.
Mary, merciful mother,
I do now pray for succour.
I want us to be happy.

let her go to the church

3188. Oh dear Mary, joy to thee,
And honour now, forever.
Be my help, blessed Mary.
In this world, give me succour.
I have no children, Mary,
Save this one. Oh watch over
Him, and see to his safety.
I trust in thee forever.

The Son *(to King Massen)*

3196. Hail to you, my dear lord King.
I have come, understanding
It is really my duty.
At any time, as you wish,
You may entrust your service
Freely for wages to me.

The King

3202. Welcome, my loyal servant.
To the wilderness you're sent
Right away, to do some sport.
Everyone now take to arms.
A tyrant's causing alarm
In the country. Don't be caught!

He goes down with armed men

Here the Tyrant shall parade, saying:

The Tyrant
3208. I am a Tyrant without
Equal, prince under the sun.
Though mad and rough men, no doubt,
Will fight me, there is no-one
To oppose me.
To the wilderness I'll go,
To have some sport. Let's go now,
Both the lordly and the low.
Prepare ye to go with me.

First Soldier of the Tyrant
3217. O my dear lord of great might,
We are ready for the sight
Of the wilderness. Let's go.
All of your greyhounds are leashed.
We have hundreds, all harnessed
Together in arms — that's so.

Second Soldier of the Tyrant
3223. And here are the little hounds.
Five loins of beef, several pounds
Of mince they'd eat in two days.
Lonkylo and Lap Keryn,
Scurel werly, yellow and thin,
Blackbird, Labol, let's see your face.

let him go down

The King
3229. Now hunter, quick, look around.
May you have joy if you've found
Some game. Unleash thy hounds now.
I see a great crowd of folk.
I'm afraid of them — no joke.
They're a Godless lot, I know.

The hart ready in the wood

The King's Second Hunter
3235. Halt! I can now see a hart.
Very soon now, he shall part
With his life, for fear of man.
Lord King, be not unwary.
The Tyrant has certainly
Risen against you. He can
Overthrow you.

The King
3242. He shall be answered, my man.
Let's wait here, soldiers, and plan
The way forward, all anew.

(and the hart hunted)

Here the torturers shall parade

First Torturer
3245. Comrades, let us not be slack.
The Tyrant, he does not lack.
He's gone to the wilderness.
Better to go after him,
Or we shall be blamed. It's grim,
But we'll be chastised, I guess.

Second Torturer
3251. If he has sent word to us,
We'll do our duty — no fuss.
Better to attend on him.
Don't know whether he's gone home.
That dirty boy of ours some
Spying might do. We'll send him.

Third Torturer
3257. Yes, quick, let us send our boy,
That speedy chap, with a ploy

To find whether he's gone home.
And let him come to warn us.
They say his servants' reward is
Fairly poor, or so say some.

First Torturer
3263. It matters not if we're slack.
We can't bring the bacon back
Or pay rent on his wages.
If he cannot be better
As a lord to us, never
Will he keep his own pages.

Second Torturer
3269. Boy, you're the biggest rascal
We've got. See if you can tell
Whether the Tyrant will go
Into the wilderness. Warn
Us where he might soon be gone,
So that we can say hello.

Third Torturer
3275. Be careful. Don't go too far.
And now, let's all drink a jar
Or two, my gentle comrades.
Tobias has gone away:
God's curse on his vile body.
He's one in a thousand rogues.

*let the three torturers pass into the tent of the
Woman's Son close by*

The Menial
3281. So the errand shall be done.
You'll not be gladder, for one,
By knowing that.

let him go down

Sir Tyrant, all your pages
Won't go without their wages,
One step from home, and that's flat.

The Tyrant
3287. What! Has it now come to that?
I shall fetch them with the flat
Side of a piece of ash stick.
We shall see how quick they'll come,
'Specially with a sore bum.
Right and left, a little prick.
Now come to me, all and some.
We'll see who can do the trick.

The Menial
3295. So now, on my way.
Sir Tyrant, I say —
That was very good counsel.
Behold, the rods are ready.
Let them be paid, and spare ye
Not, for their cheek and trouble.

The Tyrant   (*at the torturers' tent*)
3301. Now, sirs, anyone at home?
A nest without an egg. Gone,
Like yeomen in their arbour.
Now, where could they have got to?
By Mahound, puissant God, oh,
My grief, it turns to anger.

The Menial
3307. Oh, I will take you to them.
Sure, drinking in a tavern,
Are they, with their mouths all red.
Lord, please allow me to say,
I'd give them a hiding. They
Would find their buttocks half dead.

he shouts in another tent

3313. Ho masters! Is there a drink
        For me? Tell you what I think.
        I think I've got some fresh news.
        Your affairs are improving.
        By my faith, there are going
        To be wages, so it goes.
        If there's a bit
        Now, let's have it
        From the bottle — warm my toes.

First Torturer
3322. Ah, welcome home, old guzzler.
        And what says the old rotter?
        Do I need to go to him?
        Come nearer and try the pot.
        It shall cost thee but a groat
        Before we part, in good time.

Second Torturer
3328. By God, we have drunk too much.
        Too many to be paid. Such
        Is our master. God curse him.
        He's a rascal about to pay.
        To argue with him, I say,
        Is no good. Our chance is slim.

Third Torturer
3334. Hey, slave, so why did you not
        Bring our wages home here, what?
        We shall never get along
        Without our wages. A lot
        Of silver nobles, a pot
        Of money — or am I wrong?

The Tyrant

3340. Well now, I shall pay the shot,
On pain of losing the lot,
By my soul, you shan't all laugh.
Now, Tobias, come, help me,
Until they all say sorry.
Take the rod by the shaft!

the Tyrant and the Menial beat the Torturers

First Torturer

3346. What? What are you doing there?
God's curse on Tobias, I fear
He has gone and deceived us.
O lord, grant us your favour.
We didn't think that they were
Going to turn out like this.

Second Torturer

3352. O my lord, beat me no more!
Our limbs are broken and sore.
We'll never get right again.
Mischief on Tobias, for
He has been a real traitor.
Woe! Alas! Oh, I'm in pain.

Third Torturer

3358. Lord, leave me at least my life.
I beg pardon — oh what strife —
For being remiss to thee.
God's curse upon that bad boy.
He was too quick with his ploy
To give us all injury.

The Tyrant

3364. So, now you have your rewards.
If I fetch you, the word is,

You will soon be very sick.
Now, come to the wilderness.
Quick now — and that's all there is.

Demon

3369.　Peace, I order, wild and tame!
I say, Moufras is my name,
And I never feel ashamed
To do evil.
Of servants I have many,
Doing evil busily:
They all end up in my jail.

Second Demon

3376.　Through thine ingenuity,
Thou hast subtle trickery:
But I am worse.
Now, my name is Skirlywit,
Scurrilous and full of shit:
Yes — and very good at verse.

First Demon

3382.　Right: let's go to the temple.
The Tyrant will make simple,
Bad sacrifice,
So that he may do evil.
Cast him one glance, though that will
Not be to his advantage.

he descends to the temple

Tyrant

3388.　Sirs, come ye to the temple.
This is not a thick, simple
God. He deserves much honour.　　　　*(all kneel)*
There is a whitish bull's head.
I'll offer that up instead
Of this. I am thy son, O Father.

147

The Black Mass

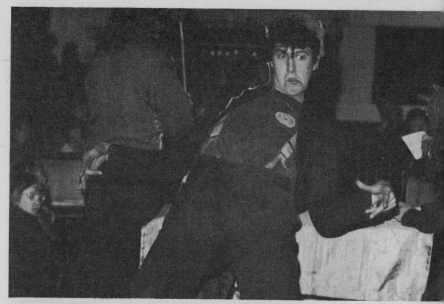

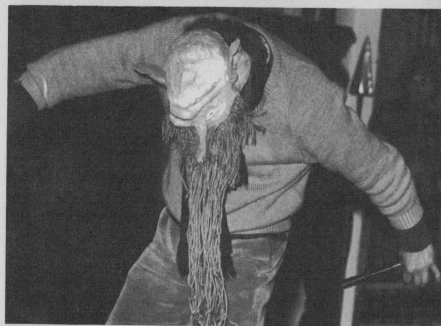

One of the Dogs of Hell

First Torturer
3394. I won't be stubborn, Mahound.
Take this ram's head I have found.
His little horns are gilded.
Now, this is so well-scented,
By thy nostrils I'll tilt it.

Second Torturer
3400. For my God, a horse's head.
In the box and no more said —
Worthy present.
With butchers' skewers on it,
I would get ninepence for it.
On this dolly it's well spent.

Third Torturer
3406. To my God, the blessed Jove,
I offer three ravens, lovely
And round are they, and quite fat.
Yes — they might be worth sixpence.
I fetched them yesterday, hence
From the moors, while on horseback.

The Menial
3412. To my God Jove, in his face,
Here's a tom-cat: there, your grace.
There is no better mouser.
I have brought him from Morville,
Annointed by the Devil.
Now take these all to you, sir,
Buck's head, skinned goat, ah this will
Please you, my God, forever.

and all the torturers sing

The Demon
3420. Now, here's a left-hand blessing.
Evil and misfortune bring,
Go and use them.

Go, pillage men who are poor.
The curses of your neighbour
Will make you think you're in heaven.

First Torturer
3426. Well now, let us all go forth.
Holy Father of the North
Has giv'n us
His best, marvellous blessing.
And now, as to pillageing,
We are commanded, I guess.

Second Torturer
3432. There is an itch in my arms,
To be sinning. It alarms
Me if I can't.
Come on, traitor,
Come on, swindler!
Get away from me you shan't.

Third Torturer
3438. Yes, we don't care where we go.
We may never return; so
Our relatives often hope.
As our nearest and dearest
Are likely to get their wish,
We'll be glad and never mope.

Second King's Huntsman
3444. My Lord, I have just warned you,
A Tyrant's risen, it's true,
And he wishes you great harm.
Behold him in the meadow
With a host. Sound the alarm!

The King
3449. Everybody, take to arms!
No cause for fear or alarm.
We shall come off the better.

The Tyrant is a heathen,
And he often likes moving
Against me and making war.

3455. Nevertheless,
He's very dense.
I'll answer him with reason.
And if he will
Meddle more still:
I'll spear him for his treason.

to the stall with two streamers

The Tyrant
3461. Ho sirs! Oh, what an array!
Tell to me, without a nay,
Who has given you licence
To come here upon my ground
To hunt the lord's beasts around?
On pain of death sir, go hence.

The King
3467. Sir Tyrant, go on your way.
Never will there come a day
When you are born to kingship.
Halt! Don't venture much nearer.
I am lord of the ground here,
These twenty years. No more lip!

Tyrant
3473. Sir Prince, are you over there?
I think that it were better
To withdraw and beseech grace.
If we come to fighting here,
One of us two, I do fear,
Will soon lose his laughing face.

The King
3479.   Now, by him that Judas sold,
       I care not for thy words bold,
       Not one blind bean.
       Never am I thy vassal.
       I shan't have any hassle
       From you, now let that be seen.

3485.   Don't accuse me
       Of falsehood — see?
       And if you do,
       I'll repay thee
       Scrupulously.
       I'll do it before I go.

The Tyrant
3491.   False whoreson, insult me not!
       I'll have thee hung and forgot,
       And all thy whelps.
       I'll have the blood of thy heart
       Spilt right here, before we part;
       Before nightfall, if it helps.

The King
3497.   That does not stand in thy power,
       You, ungodly as you are,
       Upholder of unbelief,
       By the Lord Christ of mercy,
       No better than a hound, see?
       Deny your wickedness, thief.

3503.   Yes, I will
       Thy own blood spill
       On the ground, friend.
       Don't ever start,
       Or try insult
       On the Christians.

The Tyrant

3509. Fie on thee and thy nation.
Fie a thousand times Christians.
Deny thy faith,
Or thou and all that are there
Shall die, by Satan, right here,
Through pain, misfortune and death.

The King

3515. We'll deny our faith never,
Never, not for any fear
Of thee, O thou godless Jew.
I'll maintain the faith of Christ
On the meadow, I've no fright,
No, nor any fear of you.

The Tyrant

3521. Out! Out! Charles, Beaumont, Hector!
Everyone now, go to arms.
The Devil's executor
When you're dead, and no alarm.
When it comes to conclusion,
Seize the worms for me, seize them,
And down to the ground with them.
False, false, foul foul Christians.

The King

3529. Oh, your beards are going to shake
Before you do that, traitor.
Armed folk are ready to make
An answer to you. Therefore,
Come when you will.
Soldiers, strike at them, strike sore!
I'll never obey a Jew,
Never, if I'm rich or poor.

here they shall fight

153

King Massen
3537. Oh, woe, need there is to flee,
Otherwise, dead now are we.
Oh, this time we are too weak.
Some are clearly taken
By the Godless Jew, shaken
Is my country — I can't speak.

let him pass home

The Tyrant
3543. Fare you well, O royal soldiers.
They've fled afar — it's over.
Haven't we seized anyone?

Third Soldier of the Tyrants
3546. There's a young man over there.
Right! I've got him by the hair.
Yes! Now we shall have some fun.

*(let him take
the Woman's Son)*

The Tyrant
3549. Now fare thee well, gentle knight.
He'll certainly pay his weight
In gold before he's set free.
And he shall deny his faith,
Or in prison he'll stay safe,
In the stocks. Leave it to me.

The Son
3555. That is what I will not do.
I won't deny Christ Jesu,
Whatever you do to me.
In spite of thy teeth, I shall
Worship Him as I know how,
Who made holiday and Sunday.

The Tyrant

3561. Well — if you won't deny Him,
Then you shall go to prison.
Hey, you jailers, you come here!
Put this man in prison.
If he denies not the Son
Of Mary, he shall rot there.

he goes up in his chariot

A Jailer

3567. Sir Tyrant, thy will we'll do.
Come forward to me, man, to
Lie in my nice old prison.
You've been a bit too haughty.   *(to the Woman's Son)*
You've made the Tyrant angry.
You'll be sorry you're the one.

A Boy

3573. We shall go and fetter him,
Yes, so he shan't move a limb,
Neither a hand nor a foot.
Pity that you did resist.
You'll rot here if you persist.
You'll have neither drink nor food.

Messenger   *(to the Son's Mother)*

3579. Hail to thee, O good woman.
Let me warn you of one thing.
Your son, he has been taken —
Yes — by that Godless Tyrant.
I don't know what can or can't
Be done for him. You're shaken.

The Woman

3585. Alas, my heart is broken.
I have no child nor hope in

This world but he — my solace.
Well — I serve none but Mary:
With a sick heart, I shall see
If there is hope in all this.

let her pass to the church of the Blessed Mary

she kneels and waits in the same place

3591.   Mary, dear Mother and Maid,
I do beseech thee fully,
Give to my son all your aid,
And please restore him to me.
Mary, I have served thee, prayed
With all my power, earnestly.
Blessed Mary, I obeyed
You. Break his bonds — just for me.
Mary, if you do as I said,
He'll be delivered, surely.

Tyrant
3601.   Ho, jailers, listen to me!
Pain of hanging and drawing,
Neither food nor drink give ye
To the lad I'm sending
To prison. Do you hear me?
Tomorrow, I'll be hanging,
Drawing and quartering him — see?
I hope you get my meaning.

Jailer   *(to the Tyrant)*
3609.   Lord, thy will shall now be done.
He shall never be feasted.
Oh yes — I know that, for one.
If he be hanged tomorrow,
I shan't waste food nor sorrow.
I know what has to be done.

The Woman

3615. Mary, I have besought thee
So many times for my son.
Mary, you seem not to be
Willing to help me. No-one,
Mary, helps or comforts me.
I have been crying so long.
Mary, if there is mercy,
Tonight, oh where have you gone?

3623. Mary, there's nothing for it.
My prayer avails me nothing.
Mary, I don't have the wit
To think, my Son in bonds, struggling.
Mary, believe me, I'm fit
For nothing: O my son bring
To me. Well then, yours shall quit
This place. He'll be my foundling.

3631. Mary, let go with thine arm.
Let me have thy son Jesu.
Peril nor sin shall alarm
Me now. With me home he'll go.
Come, come, baby.
Goodbye, Mary, oh, goodbye.
With my prayers I'll not annoy
Thee anymore — no, you'll see.

let her go home with Jesu

3639. Jesus Christ, oh joy to thee.
Thou shalt be kept preciously,
Just like my very own boy,
Swaddled in fine clothes nicely,
Put in the coffer safely.
Now I have a greater joy.
You are locked up securely.
I'll go to rest with this ploy.

Mary *(says in Heaven)*

3647. Jesus, my lovable son,
Without fail, everything done
Upon the earth, thou knowest.
And you know what's in the heart.
I like to be a comfort
To my servants, east and west.

Jesus

3653. O Mother, do as you please.
Who worships you shall have ease,
Though they tarry for a time.
See thy servant.
Do what is meant,
And all the will of thy mind.

Mary descends with two angels to the prison

Mary

3659. Well now, young man, how are you?
Great is your distress, you know,
It's undeserved.
He who in his life is good,
Shall live in the grace of God.
That will provide his reserve.

The Son

3665. O Lord Jesu, please help me.
I can't help it — I can't see.
I am blinded by whiteness.
Everlasting righteousness —
Oh what is all this brightness?
It's all around me — whiteness.

Mary

3671. Oh take comfort and rise up.
Thou art faint and weak, but sup
You shall and be comforted.

Now, do not be downhearted
Tonight. You shall be parted
From this prison — home instead.

The Son
3677.   Cross of Christ, benedicte!
Oh, who has come here to me,
The doors all shut firm and fast?
Just now, it was a dark night,
And now, everywhere is light.
There is a radiance at last,
Fallen around me, so bright:
A woman, queen in its midst.

Mary
3685.   Take your legs from these fetters.
Now, take them out together.
I will help you.
I'll open the doors for thee,
Without fail. Now you shall see,
Keys shall never exclude me,
And you will find that is true.

3692.   Now son, go to thy mother,
And say, without an error,
That Mary has set you free.
Say especially to her,
She must bring back my Son, where
She found him. After that, there
She must serve me, and daily.

The Woman's Son
3699.   Mary, oh worshipped be thou!
Mary, how could I be now
Fit to be guided by you?
Mary, oh my gratitude!
Mary, I'd have been destroyed
If not for thee, and it's true.

Mary

3705. Blessings, and no exception;
And your mother I mention.
Now, say this much, please, to her:
Though it would seem I should be
So far from her, yet, you see,
I would never forget her.

let Mary pass to Heaven

The Jailer

3711. Oh, woe to us, mate, get up!
Tonight, all the world erupts
With fire. The prison's gone up
In flames. Blazing!
I think a prisoner's broke out.
It's amazing!

The Boy

3717. The prisoner's gone away.
The doors were all shut, I say.
Who the devil has been here?
Let's go to the Tyrant, then.
Oh, God's curse in the kitchen!
He's a wicked man, that's clear.

The Jailer   *(to the Tyrant)*

3723. O Tyrant, woe, woe to us!
The prisoner's got away, just
This minute, this very night,
About him, a radiance.
We never had any chance
Of catching him. Oh, the fright!

The Tyrant

3729. Woe is me! Haroo! Haroo!
Oh where has my prisoner gone?
And you shall be dead, you two,
If he's escaped everyone.

By my dear soul!
You whoresons were drunk, weren't you?
You allowed the people to
Deliver him, yes, I know.

The Boy
3737. No, Tyrant, go on thy way.
God's curse upon thee. They say,
Without mincing any words,
He was taken by Mary,

And that it was certainly
You who were to blame, I heard.
They say that your cruelty
Was to blame for it, I heard.

a staff ready

The Tyrant
3745. What? What? Is that what they say?
May evil mischief get you!
If you are going to say
That I myself am too cruel,
Then let's see!
We shall put it to the test.
Then God shall be our witness.
People *shall* speak ill of me!

he beats them

The Son   *(he goes up to his mother)*
3753. Be comforted, my mother.
Reverence to dear Mary.
If we did not worship her,
It would be wrong, that I see.
I'm fortunate,
For she has delivered me
Out of prison, made me free.
I was in a dreadful state.

The Woman
3761. Be thou worshipped, O Mary!
My spirit's revived to see
My dear son now standing here.
Thou wast delivered, made free,
But tell me how — I can't see
How you can have gone from there.

The Son
3767. Mary came to me at night,
Yes — right into the prison,
With so much noise and so much light
I just could not determine
If I did sleep,
Or if I was awake then.
She really unchained me and
She held the door wide open.
She sent me to you. Don't weep.

3776. She said: "Just tell thy mother
That I have to deliver
Thee right out of the prison;
And that she must now restore
To me my very own Son."

The Woman
3781. Thanks be to blessed Mary.
If she did come and help thee,
You'll not be disappointed.
I did take her small baby
From her own statue, you see,
Because you were not restored
To me by her.
I was so sick in my heart;
And now, quickly I'll depart,
And the baby will I bear,
Quickly, quickly to the church.

Here it is wrapped up no worse
Than I would do for you. O
Mary, much joy to thee, O
Mary, much thanks to thee. So,
You did let my dear son go.

she goes down with the image of Jesus to the
church of Blessed Mary

3797. Mary, please do take thy child.
Mary, I have been quite wild
Regarding you.
But I beseech thy mercy.
One of thy servants I'll be
Forever; and that is true.

let her go home

End of the third play

FOURTH PART   MERIASEK PLAY

A Madman,   *(fighting and swaying about)*

3803.   You false people, out on you!
        Why have you put me in chains?
        I'll break your lousy heads too,
        When you let go of my reins.

Head of a Family

3807.   Talk like that now if you like.
        You won't be able to strike,
        For you are properly chained.
        To Meriasek I shall
        Take you, and very soon now.
        He'll soon heal your poor complaint.

Madman

3813.   Well then, tell me, old Big-eye,
        Who's this Meriasek guy?
        So may the devil burn thee.

Head of a Family

3816.   Meriasek, joy to thee.
        A crazy man is with me.
        People have given advice
        That I should bring him to thee,
        That you are so very wise.

Bishop Meriasek

3821.   Jesu, Lord that art above,
        Help weak and strong with thy love.
        A piteous sight is this,
        To see a man so tough,
        Yet chained. Oh what is amiss?

Madman

3826. If I wasn't so chained up
And you came a bit nearer — what?
I would knock off your blockhead.
And I would take
Your little leg
And tear it off, you clot.

Meriasek   *(kneels)*

3832. Lord Jesu, I beseech thee,
Give help now to this poor man.
Jesu Christ, gracious Lord free,
Restore his wits if you can.
Jesu, Virgin's Son, you see
Who is his enemy. Ban
Him from this man and be
My help and comfort in this plan.

3840. O thou man, wait for me there.
In the name of Mary's son,
I will unbind thee. Don't fear
Me. May he who has undone
The ills of others, help here.
Now let us pray, everyone.

Madman

3846. Great honour to Christ Jesu,
And Meriasek, to thee.
Christ brought my wits to rescue,
Through Meriasek, for me.
Meriasek, my life through,
I shall be thy devotee.
Meriasek, I'll revere thee too.
I am bound to honour thee.

he ends

Meriasek

3854. And now to my oratory
I'll go to pray to Mary,
Just to help me,
And to keep me at all times
From temptation, and such crimes
As evil thoughts I forsee.

he kneels at the oratory

3860. O Jesus, Lord, full of Grace,
Worship to thee and joy.
Jesu, Lord in every place,
O let my soul never cloy,
Nor my body.
Blessed Mary, pure virgin,
Be my succour, free from sin,
Mary, whom I love much, in
My behalf, to dear God pray.

Jesus

3869. Go to the world, angels good.
Of all Heaven, let the food
Be given to
Meriasek. He shall be
Nourished, for blessed is he.
His works are pleasing me so.

Michael

3875. Jesu, thy will shall be done.
We shall go quickly, each one,
To comfort him in person.
This is the best.
Nourishment take
There, for Christ's sake,
By the Creator's request.

the descend   *organs or singing*

Gabriel

3882.   Meriasek, joy to thee.
Almighty Christ has sent me
To give thee now some comfort.
Though you were long at fasting,
Nourishment everlasting
Shall be yours, I must report.

Sumens cibum cum laudibus divinis epulis quotidie sentit se refectum

(Taking sustenance with praises of God,
every day he feels himself refreshed with sumptuous food).

Meriasek

3888.   Jesu, of earth and Heaven Lord,
Be thou worshipped forever.
Jesu Christ, no grief afford
To those who serve thee, ever.
Jesu, I give thanks. My board
Is furnished by Heaven's saviour.
Jesu, Lord, I give my word,
Of fasting, I've no horror.

End of Part Four

THIRD PART   LIFE OF SILVESTER

Here, a Duke, ie the First Magician, shall parade

Duke
3896. I am a lord without peers,
A Duke and astronomer.
It is my duty, it appears,
To go hunting far and near.
So I will go.
I'll take some companions good.
The Bishop said that he would
Meet me along the way, too.

A Duke, ie. the Second Magician
3904. We ought to be quite wary.
There is a dragon, very
Nasty too, in that cave there.
If we come up against her,
We'll be dead, lord and pauper.
It's better to be wise here.

Huntsman   *(to the Dukes the Magi)*
3910. There are some armed people here,
And archers with bows. It's clear
They're quite able to slay her.
With my hounds I'm not afraid,
Unless they're gorged, and they're made
Much too stupid to tear her.

he goes down with armed men

Here the Bishop of Apollo shall parade

169

Apollonian Bishop

3916.   I'm every inch a bishop,
And a prelate of great worth.
Last month, I promised to stop
At the meadows, on the north
Side there, to meet Duke Magus,
The magician. Wisdom, birth
And breading he has. Let us
Go now, crozier-bearer.

Apollonian Bishop's Crozier-Bearer

3924.   I am ready, my good Lord.
It's bad management, by my word,
It is, that we can't first dine.
I'll have an empty paunch, then.
God's curse in the kitchen!
The food's meagre here, not fine.

they go down

Apollonian Bishop

3930.   Hail, O noble Duke Magus.
Crozier-bearer, Praesagus
And I have come for some sport.
Let's not keep to the low land.
There's a dragon over there, and
A big one. We shall get caught.

First Magician Duke

3936.   Now welcome, Father Bishop.
The dragon won't come, I hope:
Nowhere near us.
If she comes in sight, I know,
People will soon overthrow
Her with a lot of fuss.

here the Dragon ready in the open space

Second Magician Duke

3942. Oh, let us not trust to that.
Let's get away from the brat.
Oh no! It's coming this way.
We shall be killed — that's the truth —
By the flames coming from her mouth.
She would a thousand men slay.

here a gun ready in the Dragon's mouth and fire

First Duke

3948. Ho! Strike at her! Strike at her!
Now some are swallowed by her!

some of the soldiers swallowed

What shall we do? What a stir!
May Mahound confound you,
Filling the place with your poo.
Oh no, look. Oh, look at her!

Apollonian Bishop

3954. Oh woe to us. Let us flee,
Otherwise, quite dead are we,
By the body of Mahound.
Let us the Emperor see,
And tell Constantine that we
Think the fault is his, we've found.

First Duke

3960. Hail, Emperor Constantine.
Out on thee, out on thee, out!
Undone is thy country fine,
And by thy doing, no doubt,
Many are dead.
The great dragon in the cave
Won't let anyone pass, save
She strikes him right down, like lead.

Apollonian Bishop

3968. It's been bad in this country
Since that Christianity
Became your religion. Curse
That man who converted you.
I tell you, and this is true:
All Christ's people come off worse.

Constantine

3974. Oh my lords, go on your way.
Christ and His Mother, Mary,
Will always come to help us.
Come here, my dear Messenger.
Send quickly for Silvester.
There's something I should discuss.

Messenger *(to Constantine)*

3980. Constantine, Lord without par,
I will bring dear Silvester
Right here for you tomorrow.
Beetles won't sleep underfoot,
Nor shall I ever eat food,
Until I speak with him now.

3986. Silvester, oh joy to thee. *(to Silvester)*
Now it is necessary
To come to the Emperor,
For he wants to speak to thee,
A bit confidentially.

Silvester *(Silvester goes down)*

3991. I will come to Constantine.
He's your lord and he is mine,
And very great is his might.

(to Constantine)

Lord Emperor, joy to you.
I've come without more ado.
I would not wait long tonight.

Emperor Constantine

3997. There is an awesome dragon,
Slaying folk without reason,
Yes, and without number too.
Everyone is blaming me.
They say I cause it, really,
Through my baptism, that's true.

Constantine goes down

Silvester

4003. Through the will of Christ above,
I'll give the dragon the shove,
So she won't do any harm.
Everyone in Rome will see
It's Christ's judgement by decree.
She will not cause more alarm.

First Magician Duke

4009. One hundred men, by my fay,
Were slaughtered in just one day,
By her alone.
If you can overcome her,
We'll turn to Christ, no bother.
But you can't do it, I own.

Silvester

4015. Now, according to my prayer,
I shall go after her.

(he kneels)

Jesus

4017. Now, Peter, please go for me
To Silvester, straight away.
Comfort him, right heartily,
And inform him carefully.
He'll vanquish her, I forsee,

Through my power, quite easily.
My heart is with him, you see.
I'll not forsake him today.

Peter

4025. O Lord, I shall do thy will.
He should not fear the peril
Of the dragon. Silvester
Will lead it like a tame lamb.
Through God's power, he will command
It to the desert for sure.

Peter descends (alone to Silvester in the open space)

4031. Dear Silvester, do be glad.
Christ Lord has certainly had
The intention to defeat
The dragon. Take thy chaplains
With thee. You shall ascertain
What God commands. Do not fret.

Silvester

4037. O Lord of Heaven, help me!
I do not know who to see
For comfort. I do not know.
Great is Jesus' power above.
I certainly trust his love.
He'll help me, wher'er I go.

Peter

4043. I am a true apostle
Of Christ, and my own loyal
Name is Peter. Do not fear.

4046. To the old Dragon speak thus:
"Jesus Christ, son of the Cross,
Born of the Virgin Mary,
Suffered upon the Cross-tree,

Buried in the cemetary;
On the third day, he rose free,
Ascended into Heaven.
On Doomsday, he'll come again,
To judge us, flesh in skin, will he.
Now, in his name, O Dragon,
Come out here at once to me."

4057.   The sign of the Cross with thee,
And you'll lead her perfectly,
According to thy will. One
Thing only: Jesus will see
That nothing at all shall go wrong.

Silvester

4062.   Oh now, blessed be the time.
I shall go forth with a hymn
To meet the Dragon out there.
Come with me, my two chaplains.
The sign of the Cross maintain
Before us, for dear Mary.

A cross ready for Silvester's first chaplain

Silvester's First Chaplain

4068.   I will truly bear the Cross
And my comrade too — no loss.
Let him bear the lit lantern.
The cave is deep where she is,
One hundred paces, I wis.
Christ keep us from darkness, this turn.

The Second Chaplain bears the lantern

First Duke ie. Magician

4074.   Oh sirs, let us go and see
What Silvester does with the she
Dragon. Wonder what he'll do.

I think that nought but magic
Would really do the right trick.
He has to use deceit, true.

Silvester *(kneels)*
4080. In the name of Mary's Son,
Jesus is the only one,
He who was dead and buried,
And raised up on the third day;
To Heaven ascended — aye,
On the right side of Father God.
He shall come, as they do say,
To judge the bad and the good.

In his name, come forth, I say,
As is commanded today,
By Christ to me in this world.

she issued from the cave

First Duke, ie. Magician
4091. The Dragon's coming — behold!
It's better for us to go.
Oh! Oh I am dying here.
Oh, her fetid breath is so
Dreadful, I shan't recover.

let him fall down in fear of the Monster

Second Duke ie. Magician
4096. She has killed me with her wind.
By Mahound, chief of the kind
Saints, get away — I can't move.
Oh, pity I didn't mind
Before. What an end to choose.

let him fall down in fear of the Monster

Silvester

4101. Stay! Stay here, O thou dragon.
In the name of Christ, dear one,
I will soon lay hold of thee,
And lead thee like a lamb, on
Through the power of God, see?

Constantine

4106. Silvester, oh praised be thou!
Thou hast quickly proven how
Christ is head of the Lords now.
That was what I really wanted.
And now, dear sirs, what say you?
A blessed man, as I said.

Apollonian Bishop

4112. Here are all the dead people.
If it's not too much trouble,
I'd like to see them alive.
Then we would believe freely
In Jesus, Son of Mary.
Great and small would then believe.

Silvester

4118. Jesus, lord of strong and weak,
Jesus, for these folk I speak.
They are on earth cast down.
Grant that they may stand up whole.
If they are wise, they will know
Their evil is overthrown.

the two dukes arise, and all

First Duke ie. Magician

4124. Silvester, worshipped be thou.
In Christ I will believe now,
That he is God of Mercy.

The Dragon's an evil beast.
A baptizer I'll beseech,
Worship the Son of Mary.

Apollonian Bishop

4130. Since I am brought to my wits,
To be baptized, I do wish,
And worship Jesus always.
The false Dragon, that reptile,
I don't wish to see her. I'll
Call her repulsive, always.

Silvester

4136. Do not have great fear of her,
Through the grace of Jesus above.
Into the wilderness far
I'll banish her, for the love
Of Jesus. Thus, in his dear
Name, I command thee to shove
Off. Go quickly away from here,
To the wilderness. Now, move.
Never do evil, take care,
To beast nor man — and for proof,
Never more return to here,
On pain of death. That's enough.

Apollonian Bishop

4148. She is surely gone away.
All of Rome is bound today
To honour dear Silvester.
Baptize us forthwith, I say,
We have seen quite openly,
There's no God but Jesus dear.

holy water ready

Silvester

4154. I baptize you together.
In the name of the Father,
And the Son, and Holy Ghost,

Amen. And now, my clergy,
To my great palace worthy,
Let us go, least and foremost.

Silvester's Second Chaplain

4160. We're ready to go with you.
Oh, there is so much to do,
And we can do so little.
Now, worship Christ at this time.
Through you are healed many fine
Souls, and brought to Christ, it's true.

Constantine

4166. Honour to Christ's salvation!
Through Silvester, here and now,
Rome's people from damnation
Are here delivered, and how!
Firstly, from their dissention
From the right road, to the true
Way; secondly, I mention
The Dragon, plague-worm, I vow.

4174. Let's all go in procession
To the court. The intention
Is to take him.
We're all bound to Silvester.
Many were devoured here
By the heathen Dragon. Fear
No more. Accompany him.

they go in procession to the Pope's palace

End of Second Play

FIFTH PART   MERIASEK PLAY

A Feeble Man or a Cripple
4181. Oh God, oh how grieved I am.
My limbs are maimed a long time.
I can't walk but on crutches.
Oh I am loathsome and weak.
Meriasek shall I seek.
I hope I have some success.

4187. I've been out during the night,
Chilled, troubled, in all my plight,
When others are home sleeping.
Head over heels in a pool,
Knees and flesh torn like a fool,
I can hardly keep standing.

4193. I have come here to this place.
A blessing on thee, Sir. Grace
Of our Lord, sweet Jesus.
Now I want to see the face
Of Meriasek gracious.

Meriasek
4198. He is speaking now with thee.
What do you wish of him — me?
Tell me forthwith.
I shall always
Attempt to ease
Poor people's needs.
That I shall give.

The Cripple

4205. I am a rotten cripple.
Meriasek, I tell
Thee, I am very needy.
For love of the Passion
Which Jesus bore for his own,
Meriasek, help me.

4211. All of my limbs are maimed.
Even death is ashamed
Of me, and he avoids me.
I cannot walk, but I slink.
People just see me and shrink.
They just don't want to see me.
Naked am I, and I think
I'm a beast of low degree.

Meriasek

4219. Jesu, who made Heaven and Earth,
I pray him, for all I'm worth,
To provide healing for thee,
To come and go as you will.
He can cure your every ill,
Without ointment — you'll soon see.

4226. Oh Jesus is our Saviour.
May he raise you up for sure,
And may Mary help thee too.
So may she grant
Thee, miscreant,
Healing, to make thy limbs new.

The Cripple

4232. Oh Lord, how I do rejoice!
To Meriasek and Christ
In thanks I do raise my voice.
My limbs restored — very nice.
Now I am quite spoiled for choice.

I'll walk or run
And have great fun.
I'll stand without thinking twice.

Bishop Meriasek
4240. It is Jesus you must thank.
Wrap this garment, head to shank,
Right around thee, my good man.
Take for yourself food and drink.
Give thanks to Christ. Always think
He gave you medicine.

The Cripple
4246. Jesus above,
The Virgin's love
Repay to thee.
Meriasek dear,
All poor men, we're
Ready to help thee with glee.

Meriasek   *(lying in the oratory)*
4252. Come to me, my bretheren.
My Lord's Body, oh amen,
I have received here today.
And so, I must depart, then,
Though the company be gay.

4257. It is Jesus I must thank.
I am touched by Death so dank.
I must needs go from this world.
Brethren, practice your goodness,
And to poor people, always
Give succour. Give me your word.

The Dean   *(to Meriasek)*
4263. Lord, how will it be for us,
If you depart? Mischievous
Is the way of life on earth.

I know for certain — no doubt —
Never a Lord hereabouts
Will be equal to thy worth.

Meriasek
4269. Now the time is drawing nigh.
To Christ will I give thanks. I
Am grateful for his goodness
In this world. I am confessed,
Anointed, houseled — I guess
I am ready, thanks to Jesu.
To Christ, the Virgin's son who
Loves us, I pray at the last.

(kneels)

4277. Who honours me on this earth,
Jesu, Lord, O grant to them
Power of being shriven, birth
To death. Oh do not condemn.
Receive Christ's body. Go forth
Anointed, ready even
For their soul to escape wrath
And go to the joy of Heaven.

4285. In the place where I may be
Honoured, I pray for those same
Few, that they may be healthy.
If they should pray in my name,
And be healed there of every
Disease and illness that came
To them, sustenance freely
They should be given, I proclaim.

4293. In Cornwall, I'll have a house
By Mary Church of Camborne.
Whoever seeks me, I'll choose
To absolve him, though unshorn.
Though my body be elsewhere,

If Jesus he has implored,
By Jesus shall he be heard,
In that same place, by my word,
If his petition is fair.

4302.　My festival will
Surely be in June,
The first Friday, till
Doomsday; so festoon
Me then. My blessing
With the good blessing of Christ,
Head of the angels, yea thrice
For those who keep this founding.

A Canon
4310.　Meriasek, how are you?
Apart from weakness, it's true,
You seem to be more at ease.
Oh, we may be so mournful
For thee, it may be awful
If you leave us, I forsee.

Meriasek
4316.　On Friday, Christ Jesu, dear,
Oh, he did die for us all.
On a Friday, I've no fear
Of giving up my own soul,
To my Saviour.
And therefore, on a Friday,
Be that festival, aye
Held by you all, evermore.

4324.　Brethren, draw nearer here.
In token of all my love,
I will kiss you all, and fear

Not in the name of God above.
Let us part now, in good cheer.

4329. Into thy hands, O Lord,
I commend my spirit.

And so he sent forth his spirit
The Holy Ghost, ready from Heaven to fetch the Soul, and the Soul ready.

Jesus
4331. Angels, fly to earth for me,
To fetch me, very gently,
The soul of Meriasek.
I have granted everything
To him in the world, good things
That in his life he did seek.

Michael
4337. Oh Jesu, Heaven's kingdom
He does deserve. It's for him.
He has been a good servant.
We'll do thy will.
We shall fulfil
All that is meant.

The Holy Ghost ready and the Soul ready

Gabriel
4343. Meriasek be thou glad,
All that thou hast asked and bade,
Is now granted.
To heaven go
In gladness so,
To dwell in joy never shed.

Bishop of Cornouailles

4349. My cross-bearer, I have heard
That Meriasek, in a word,
Is *in extremis*, dying.
I will go and see whether
He's alive or dead. Never
Have I known his like. Compare
Him I can't with anything.

he goes down

Earl of Vannes

4156. I am mournful for one thing.
Meriasek now being
Quite probably on his bier,
Come with me now, all my knights.
We'll put the matter to rights.
Bury him with reverence dear.

he goes down

Second Bishop

4362. And now the Lords are surely
For Meriasek ready.
They will put him in the earth.
Oh God, take care of his soul.
There won't be another in all
Brittany. This I do see.

he goes down

Earl of Vannes

4368. Joy to you, O worthy Lord.
Have you all yet heard the word,
Meriasek passed away?
As I believe, you are bound
To put him in the ground,
And we likewise, as they say.

187

Bishop of Cornouailles

4374. Oh yes, Sir Earl, yes indeed.
I believe it is agreed,
And our part is
To go with true reverence
And bury him at our expense,
That loyal servant of Jesus.

Earl Globus goes down

Second Bishop

4380. Joy to you all and much grace.
I am satisfied with the place
And the company. At this time,
Meriasek has departed.
May joy, through Jesus, be granted,
To his soul in the Sublime.

4386. Yes, he was a worthy man,
From the day his life began,
As we know in Brittany.
To know him was a privilege.
Many a grief did he assuage.
I saw proof of his message.
He worked miracles for me.

4393. I was blind many a year,
Yet I could not find nor hear
Of a man who could cure me.
But when I came here to him,
Through the power of Christ in Heaven,
He restored my sight completely.
Thanks to Jesus, oh amen,
He saved me from misery.

Bishop of Cornouailles

4401. A great many men have found
That they are forever bound
To Meriasek, and they

Worship him. He is a saint
In Heaven, without any taint,
After his work here, for aye.

Earl of Vannes   *(to the Dean)*
4407.   May God save all the college.
Sir Dean, will you please tell us,
Is Meriasek passed away?
It is said in this country,
That his soul has gone to joy,
So I believe as they say.

The Dean
4413.   O Lord, he has passed away.
His soul with the Trinity
Has gone, so I do believe.
No fairer end in this world
Was ever made, by my word.
I do not think we should grieve.

The Canon
4419.   Meriasek, he said mass
On the Friday morning last,
Glorious and fair.
And after that, then he said
He was touched by death, and fled
Home to Jesus, without care.

The procession ready and two censers

4425.   From Christ he besought one thing,
One thing only desiring
For whoever worships him.
To himself he called us all,
And commanded us, both small
And great, to come and kiss him.

4431. His two hands he did upraise.
       On the true God he cried "praise,"
       Then to Heaven turned his gaze,
       Joyous in everyone's sight.
       The verse, *in manus tuas*
       He said, not pausing. Alas,
       When it was ended, his bright
       Soul then he resigned at last
       To merciful God on high.

The Canon

4440. There are only some who know
       His converse in the world. Though
       He wore some good cloth outside,
       He wore a shirt of horsehair
       Next to his body; and ne'r
       Rested any night. He sighed
       Not in blankets, no, nor sheet.
       The rough straw itself was meet.
       Not long in bed did he bide.

The Dean

4449. Like he was, worshipping Christ,
       To dear St. John the Baptist.
       He drank not cider nor wine.
       A thousand times in the night,
       He went down on his knees quite,
       To worship Jesus divine.

4455. And a thousand times a day,
       On his two knees perfectly,
       Was his mortification.
       And therefore did his knees swell
       So badly that you could tell
       He had difficulty standing.

The Canon

4461. Always praying or reading,
       He was, proceeding
       To say nothing but goodness.

So, nourished with angels' food
I believe he was, in good
Faith, or he could not progress.

The Earl of Vannes
4467. This is a very great loss
Here in Brittany, to us.
Masters, if you are ready,
To the church we shall now go,
To put the body below
The ground, quickly.

The Dean
4473. Everything is ready here,
And all arranged is the choir,
As meet for a worthy man.
People from all the country
Round are coming. Loved was he
Above all others, this Christian.

The Earl of Vannes
4479. Yes, he deserved to be loved.
Many people it behoved
Him to comfort; all the weak,
The blind and the deaf, the maimed,
The palsied, lepers the same:
How many, we can't bespeak.

The Dean
4485. Let us all go, in God's name,
And in Mary's, I proclaim.
Please, all help with the coffin.
Let us go into the church.
May Jesus grant that we search
To do good works, and often.

The Earl of Vannes
4491. Now, I will carry one end.
No man was loved more, I contend,
No, not by me on this earth.
He was filled with such goodness
And also with blessedness.
Yes, his time was of great worth.

Earl Globus
4497. I will bear the other end.
Meriasek, I contend,
Healed me, blind, without a friend.
I shall always worship him,
As I am thus bound to do,
And shall, all my life through,
'Til with age my eyes grow dim.

The Dean
4504. Now let sing all the clergy,
In the name of God's mercy.
And let us all go quickly,
For he deserved
To be honoured
In this country.

here they sing

Second Bishop
4510. Now prepare ye all the tomb,
As it is meet, in Christ's name,
That we may soon bury him.
It is the due of a worthy
Man such as he, oh truly.
He gave goodness to many.
To Jesus we sing our hymn.

The Naked Man
4517. The tomb is made here by me,
As I am bound, you'll agree,
To serve him while in this world.

I was maimed, and a leper,
But he healed me, so clever
Was he. I love him, my Lord.

The Cripple
4523. The tomb is now cleansed by me,
My Lords, as you will now see.
Do as you will.
Oh God, how we do regret
To see him dead, and let
Him go to the earth so chill.

Bishop of Cornouailles
4529. God's will is not to resist,
So let us all now assist
The body into its grave.
And so now, in God's name,
I'll say the benediction,
On behalf of Jesus brave.

Earl of Vannes
4535. Into the tomb I'll put him.
Keep his cloak in the dear name
Of Mary's Son. Keep it for me.
Behold, the body lying.
Whether servant or a king,
We all come to this, I see.

Bishop of Cornouailles
4541. May the Lord of Heaven bless him.
My children, let's cover him,
In dear God's name.
And let us go home from here.
Grieving hurts me now, I fear:
Others too, it would appear,
They feel the same.

Earl of Vannes

4548. Peace, in the name of God above,
To all who are gathered here.
Meriasek's Life we strove
To set before you, clear
As we could in these two days.
Now, whoever puts his trust
In him, and prays, well, they must
Find, Jesus is not unjust.
He'll grant them their desire — don't fear.

4557. Meriasek's blessing to you,
Sweet Mary of Camborne too.
The blessing of the apostles free.
We do beseech you, one and aye,
Drink, all of you, with the play,
Before going to some hostelry.

4563. Pipers all, now start to blow,
We shall all put on a show
And start to dance.
So, go or stay,
Welcome today —
Or leave here a week hence!

The Director

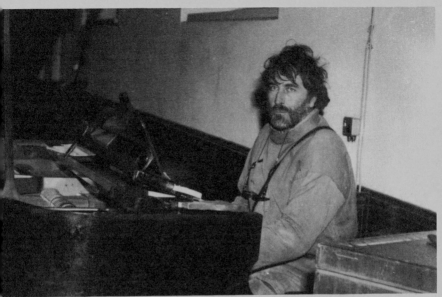

The Musicians

REFERENCES AND SUGGESTED READING LIST

COMBELLACK, M. "A Scholar's Prayer" in 'British Poetry: A Short Anthology,' *Pacific Quarterly*, III, 4, (Oct. 1978), 419.

HARRIS, M. The Life of Meriasek, a Medieval Cornish Miracle Play, Washington:1977

SOUTHERN, R. The Staging of Plays Before Shakespeare, London: 1973.

STOKES, W. (ed.) *Beunans Meriasek: The Life of St Meriasek, Bishop and Confessor: A Cornish Drama,* London: 1872.

THOMAS, C. Christian Antiquities of Camborne, St. Austell: 1967.

TURK, F A. & COMBELLACK, M. "Doctoring and Disease in Medieval Cornwall; exegetical notes on some passages in 'Beunans Meriasek'," *Cornish Studies* IV − V, (1976−7), 56−76.

WELLWORTH, G. E. "Methods of Production in the Medieval Cornish Drama," *Speech Monographs* XXIV (1957), 212−218.

WICKHAM, G. Early English Stages 1300-1600, I, London: 1963.

Cornish Language students please note: I have not included the works of R. Morton Nance in this selected bibliography because my renderings and interpretations are sometimes at variance with his, and I do not want to cause unnecessary confusion to student and director. Nance was not a medieval European dramatist, but his work as a scholar of Cornish remains unsurpassed to this day.